PROPHETIC
evangelism

PROPHETIC
evangelism

When God speaks
to those who don't know him

Mark Stibbe

Authentic

MILTON KEYNES ● COLORADO SPRINGS ● HYDERABAD

Authentic Media, 9 Holdom Avenue, Bletchley, Milton Keynes,
Bucks., MK1 1QR, UK
1820 Jet Stream Drive, Colorado Springs, CO 80921, USA
Medchal Road, Jeedimetla Village, Secunderabad 500 055, A.P.,
India
www.authenticmedia.co.uk
Authentic Media is a division of IBS-STL U.K., previously
STL UK, limited by guarantee, with its registered office at
Kingstown Broadway, Carlisle, Cumbria CA3 0HA. Registered
in England & Wales No.1216232. Registered charity 270162 and
Scotland No. SCO40064

British Library Cataloguing in Publication Data
A catalogue record for this book is available from
the British Library.

978-1-86024-457-5

Cover illustration by Koraley Orritt
Cover design by David Lund
Print Management by Adare Carwin
Printed and bound in the UK by J F Print Ltd., Sparkford, Somerset

CONTENTS

ACKNOWLEDGEMENTS

There are quite a number of people I would like to thank sincerely for their help and inspiration in the writing of this book.

I want to thank my friend J. John for his comments on the manuscript, and especially for his extraordinarily encouraging affirmation of the contents. To have such an endorsement from the UK's premier evangelist is a huge help.

I am also really thankful to all those who exercise a prophetic ministry and who have encouraged me along the way. I want to thank Bruce Collins, Graham Cooke, Marc Dupont, Sharon Stone and Doug Addison in particular. Their input has been invaluable.

I also want to thank those who have provided testimonies from their own experience, particularly Revd Greg Downes (tutor in evangelism at London Bible College), Revd Jonathan Kissell, James Roberts, Noonie Kissell, Graham Cleveland, John Wright, Adrian Clarke and Heather Godfrey – all of whom are experienced practitioners in the art of prophetic evangelism.

I am extremely grateful to Koraley Orritt for her amazing painting that forms the front cover of this book. I met Koraley and her husband Paul while leading a Prophetic Evangelism conference in Alberta, Canada. Koraley is an extremely gifted prophetic artist who uses art in evangelism. When I saw her painting of the eagle in her studio I knew straight away that this would make the perfect cover illustration. Thank you Koraley, and thank you Paul.

I want to thank Malcolm Down and the team at Authentic for doing such a swift and excellent job with the production and publication for this book.

I would also like to thank all those people that have come to one of the Prophetic Evangelism conferences I have held both in the UK and abroad. The testimonies of those who have been prepared to 'have a go' have been an inspiration to me and the teams from St Andrew's that accompanied me.

Finally, I want to thank the people at the church I serve, St Andrew's, Chorleywood. I taught a series on prophetic evangelism in August 2003 and we experienced definite growth as we explored together the use of prophesy in witnessing. Seeing God moving so powerfully in prophetic evangelism in the local church was a big encouragement to believe that this book could be a major resource for evangelising Great Britain and beyond.

FOREWORD

There appear from time to time books of unassailable merit – *Prophetic Evangelism* is such a book. True, Mark Stibbe is a dear friend, but I am judging his book by objective standards when I say that he has given us a book that instructs and inspires.

Prophetic Evangelism is tightly reasoned but brightly written. The doctrine is solid and the examples are both biblical and contemporary. The content is dramatic and absorbing. The theology is at all times practical and illustrated by powerful testimony.

Every time I read the Bible I am thankful that a few people, in God's infinite plan, recorded his word for all generations. Having said that, we need teachers who can explain Scripture, enhance it, draw inferences from it and in many ways make it more meaningful for us all. A good teacher weighs and tests, provides insights, and applies changeless truths in a variety of ways.

This is what Mark Stibbe so ably does for us in this book. He vividly explains what 'prophetic evangelism' is, using the Bible as his foundation. But this is not just Bible teaching. As I read the manuscript, on several occasions I felt Mark was like a prophet bursting in from the wilderness with a message from God; the words jolted and challenged me. *To read Mark Stibbe is not so much to read as to see.*

Evangelism is a daily activity for all Christians. From home to school, to work, to play, we are constantly sending out a message with our mouth and our actions.

Mark shows us what prophetic evangelism should be,

how it relates to our culture, where we have failed in its practice and how we can connect with those around us.

We are God's megaphone to lost people. This book will help the church to find its voice again.

J. John

INTRODUCTION

'You can't write a book on prophetic evangelism. Prophecy is for believers only! That's what the Bible says.'

So said a Christian leader who also happens to be an expert in evangelism. My heart sank. Could it really be true? Was I wrong in my understanding of Scripture? Had I been mistaken to run all those conferences both in the UK and around the world on 'prophetic evangelism'? Were all the testimonies of prophesying into the lives of unbelievers really invalid or, worse still, unbiblical?

For years now I have been convinced that God wants believers to be more and more open to receiving prophetic revelation about those who are not yet Christians. In other words, I believe that the Holy Spirit is wanting to speak through Christians to lost people, waking them up to the reality that Jesus is alive and that he knows their every thought, word and action. At the same time I am convinced that God has been wanting to speak directly into the lives of the lost, through prophetic phenomena such as dreams, visions, pictures, messages and so on. To put it succinctly, I believe that our heavenly Father wants to deploy the gift of prophecy in evangelism!

Why do I think that?

First of all, I believe it because the Bible clearly teaches it. There are many examples of God's people using prophecy in their witness to unbelievers. Even in the Old Testament there is evidence, as I will show throughout this book. Certainly Jesus used prophecy in his ministry to seekers. He saw prophetically into the lives of

Nathanael, Simon Peter, the Samaritan woman, the paralysed man who was lowered through the roof, and of course Zacchaeus – and these are just the selected highlights! After Pentecost, Jesus gave the gift of prophecy to believers as one resource among many in their witness to the world. Apostles like Peter and Paul operated in the gift of prophecy as they evangelised the lost, as the pages of the book of Acts demonstrate. In many places in the Bible we see prophetic visions, dreams, pictures, messages, impressions and even riddles used to move people from a place of unbelief to faith.

The second reason why I believe our heavenly Father wants to use prophecy in evangelism is because of my experience and the experiences of many others. Now personal experiences can be very subjective, I know. They always need to be secondary to the more objective testimony of the Bible. At the same time, you need to know that you are about to embark on a journey in this book, a journey in which you will read of many ordinary people who have received prophecies for those who did not know Christ, often with immediate and life-changing effects. Not only that, but you are going to read about unbelievers who have received revelations of Jesus through visions and dreams. This has happened to people of other faiths and no faith.

So both Scripture and experience show that our Father wants to use prophecy in evangelism.

If that is the case, why was I told that prophecy is only for believers?

The number one cause of this view is, in my opinion, a wrong interpretation of 1 Corinthians 14:22. The New International Version reads as follows: 'Tongues, then, are a sign, not for believers but for unbelievers; prophecy, however, is for believers, not for unbelievers.' This is part of a notoriously difficult passage and we will look at it in more detail in chapter 5. Let me just say at this stage that Paul is emphatically *not* saying that the church isn't to use prophecy with unbelievers. He goes on to say the following:

> But if an unbeliever or someone who does not understand comes in while everybody is prophesying, he will be convinced by all that he is a sinner and will be judged by all, and the secrets of his heart will be laid bare. So he will fall down and worship God, exclaiming, 'God is really among you!' (1 Cor. 14:24–25, NIV).

If Paul is saying 'don't use prophecy with unbelievers', he would hardly have gone on to show how life-changing it is when unbelievers are exposed to the prophetic!

So what *is* Paul saying here?

We will find out in chapter 5. But a summary of his argument would run as follows:

Prophecy (given in church worship services) is a sign primarily for believers. Its primary function is to demonstrate, to those who already believe, that God is in the house and that they are under favour. Paul goes on to say that even though prophecy is a sign primarily for believers, it can also have a secondary effect on unbelievers. It can take them very quickly from a negative to a positive view of God and his people. So even though prophecy functions as a sign to believers that 'God is among us', it can also demonstrate the same truth to unbelievers. Prophecy can be used with those who don't know Christ as well as with those who do.

Let me give you an example from my personal experience just this last week.

I arrived at Heathrow airport at 8 a.m. having prayed

that in the next twenty-four hours of travelling to New Mexico I would have divine appointments with seekers. What I didn't cater for was how quickly this prayer would be answered.

I headed for the check-in desks. I was being ushered to the first-class check-in (I wasn't travelling first class!) when I saw a nearer check-in become available and felt drawn there instead. There was a young woman in the airline's uniform; I'd say a Muslim or a Hindu in her early thirties, waiting to serve me. As I approached the desk I saw her eyes and two words came to me: 'sadness' and 'rejection'. The eyes are the window of the soul. They often reveal the secrets of a person's heart.

I approached the desk and said, 'Hi, how are you today?' Even though I was chirpy and polite, she wouldn't reply. So I carried on handing in my details. After a few minutes I decided to try again. 'Are you sure you're okay?'

At this her eyes started to well up. I then said to her, 'You're suffering from rejection, aren't you?'

At this she registered surprise and then opened up about how her boyfriend was rejecting her and how she had lived with this kind of thing for a long time. 'Everyone has rejected me in my life,' she concluded.

'God hasn't,' I replied. 'In fact, he's a perfect Father and he's crazy about you?'

'How do you know?' she asked.

I then started to share with her. I gave her a copy of my book *The Big Picture* (co-authored with J. John) and told her to look at the chapter I had written called 'In search of the Father'. She asked whether I lived nearby. I said yes and gave details of my church. She then asked if she could see me and how much it would cost! I said she could come and visit and it would be free.

She gave me her e-mail address, and I gave her mine. Then she shook my hand, looking so much brighter!

Both my study of Scripture and experiences like these have led me to the view that it is not only biblical but also urgent to reinstate prophecy to its rightful place in evangelism. I believe that God wants to speak through believers right into the hearts of unbelievers. And I also believe that God wants to speak directly into the lives of unbelievers, particularly through visions and dreams. Indeed, we will see in this book that when prophecy becomes one of the primary gifts used in evangelism, there will be a great harvest.

So this book is really a user-friendly exploration of how this happens in Scripture and in our experience today. It is the first book (to my knowledge) ever written on this subject. My prayer is that it will inspire you to use the gift of prophecy as you witness to those who don't yet know the Lord Jesus Christ. My prayer is also that you would become so wise and mature in using prophecy with seekers, that one by one you hear them say to you, 'Truly God is among you.'

Mark Stibbe, Summer 2003.

Chapter 1

WHAT IS PROPHETIC EVANGELISM?

A few years ago I had to take my car into a local garage for a service. As I stood waiting in line at the reception desk the Holy Spirit drew my attention to the young woman who was serving the customers. Sometimes this happens – the Lord highlights a person to whom I am going to minister in some way. But what I sensed the Lord saying was not a positive word. I sensed him saying, 'The young woman before you is terminally ill. She doesn't know me yet. But I want you to help her to find me.'

That was it! I went up to the counter to book my car for a service and saw from her badge that her name was Wendy, but there was no opportunity there and then to say anything to her. And in any case, what do you say when you have a word that serious? Sometimes, when the Lord speaks to you, you need wisdom about how and when to share what you receive.

Trusting that God had another time for me to minister to Wendy, I wrote her name on my heart and started to pray for her. A few months later, during the summer, I was conducting a wedding service at the church where I was a curate. Who should I see as one of the bridesmaids but Wendy! After the service, before everyone left, I managed to get alongside Wendy, who was standing with her boyfriend, a mechanic at the garage called Tony.

I told Wendy that I had seen her at the reception desk in the garage and that the Lord had told me to pray for her. She replied that she was very grateful. Even Tony said so too, adding that Wendy had a very serious illness. I told them both that they were on my heart and that they were not to hesitate to contact me if they needed prayer. I gave Tony my home phone number, stressing that he could use it any time.

Several weeks later Tony rang me. It was about 3 a.m. He told me that they had been on holiday in Scotland, that Wendy had gone into a coma and that he had driven her back home in the caravan. He shared that Wendy was now in the local hospital, not expected to survive beyond a few hours.

I rushed there to find Wendy in a bed next to various machines and surrounded by family and medics. I asked for two minutes to pray for Wendy and invited the Holy Spirit to come into that hospital side room. I don't remember particularly sensing the presence of God or seeing any reaction in Wendy as I prayed. I don't remember exactly what I prayed either, except that it was something along the lines that God had said I was to help Wendy find him and that I needed more time.

After I had prayed, I bade farewell and went home. Several hours later the phone rang. It was Tony to say that Wendy had recovered dramatically and that the nurses were baffled. The doctors had discharged her and she was now back home!

Now I would love to say that Wendy went on to recover completely and that she is alive and well today. But that did not happen. The Lord had impressed on me that he wanted her to have an opportunity to get to know him. I did not receive a word about her being healed. That has occurred on other occasions. I have prayed for several seekers who have been sick and they have been healed. But this time, with Wendy, I did not sense any leading at all that she was going to get well.

Wendy lived another four months. During that time the family invited me to go and visit her in their own home. They were all present on the day I visited. The extraordinary thing is that Wendy, not I, asked them all to leave so that we could have time on our own together. When they had all gone I told her that I had something to share. She replied that she knew, and that she knew what I was about to share. And she did! She knew it was time to get ready for heaven. There and then she confessed her sins, committed her life to the Lord Jesus Christ, and received the Holy Spirit. When Wendy died that winter I was able to tell the whole church – packed with non-Christians – that Wendy was in Paradise. Most of her colleagues from the local garage came to the Christmas services to hear the Gospel as a result of being challenged at that funeral. All this as a result of one prophetic word received in a queue at a garage reception desk!

Prophetic Evangelism Defined

This encounter with Wendy revealed to me the extraordinary power of 'prophetic evangelism'. But what do we mean by 'prophetic evangelism'? *Prophetic evangelism is simply God using revelatory phenomena to speak to the hearts of those who don't know Jesus.*

When God poured out his Holy Spirit on the Day of Pentecost, believers were given power to witness about Jesus (Acts 1:8). One of the gifts that God gave to his church that day was the gift of prophecy (Acts 2:17). Prophecy is the ability to receive and declare revelation from God. When God empowered his church to witness, he gave the gift of prophecy to help us in that task. The gift of prophecy is of immense value for evangelising the unchurched (1 Cor. 14:24–25).

Now it is important right at the start to realise that there are basically two main forms of prophetic evangelism. I will call these Type A and Type B.

Type A is where a believer receives revelation about an unbeliever. This can happen through a vision, or a dream, an impression, through any number of ways, as we will see later. In Type A the person receiving the prophetic revelation is the believer. The believer shares this revelation sensitively with the unbeliever, with the result that the unbeliever recognises that God is real, that he is alive, and that he speaks today. This of course has a huge impact on that person's openness to hearing and accepting the Gospel.

Let me give you an example.

A Christian friend of mine – a practitioner in prophetic evangelism – shared how he had rung the telephone enquiry service recently in order to find a phone number he needed. The woman on the other end sounded miserable so he encouraged her not to be unhappy. This is how the conversation unfolded:

'Why shouldn't I be unhappy?' she asked.

'Well, God cares about you, for one thing.'

'Prove it,' she replied.

My friend prayed for God to give him something.

'You are unhappy because you were engaged once.'

'So what?' she replied. 'Lots of people have been.'

At this point my friend paused and prayed: 'God, I'm on the line here' (forgive the pun). Just then the Lord revealed the name of the person to whom the woman had been engaged.

'Yes, but you were engaged to someone called David.'
The phone went silent.

'How did you know that?' she asked.

'Because God told me. Now do you believe God cares about you?'

'Yes,' she replied.

This is an example of the way in which a believer, receiving prophetic revelation for an unbeliever, causes that person to see that God is indeed alive. This is a typical example of Type A.

In **Type B** the Holy Spirit reveals something directly about Jesus to an unbeliever. This may come in the form of a vision, a dream or an impression, indeed in many varied ways. Whatever way it comes to the unbeliever, they realise as a result of this prophetic revelation that Jesus Christ is alive and that he is appealing to them to follow him. Since the essence of true prophecy is the testimony of Jesus (Rev. 19:10) the effect of this kind of revelation is to awaken the person to the truth of the Gospel. The challenge then is for the person to connect with a Christian so that the journey towards conversion can be completed.

Here is another example. A friend of mine who is now a Christian used to be a Muslim. He was brought up in the Middle East by a devout Muslim family. He was being groomed as a young man to promote Islam in the Western world using mass media technology. But while growing up in the Middle East he became aware of a lack of peace in his life.

While in England on a business trip my friend started to read a Gideon Bible in his hotel bedroom. One night, as he became more and more impressed with the Jesus he was reading about, he fell asleep and had a dream. Jesus came to him in this dream with his arms outstretched and said to him, 'I am the Way.' Jesus also revealed himself to this Muslim man as 'the Prince of Peace'.

As a result of that dream he went to a Christian church in the city, met up with a young person in a coffee shop, and heard the Gospel. This took more than one visit and more than one conversation. Not long after this he gave his life to Jesus and he is now promoting the Gospel to the Arab world in Arabic using mass media technology. Needless to say, there has been a great cost to pay in relationship to his family back home. Yet my friend believes that it is all worth it because he has a peace that the world, and indeed his own religion (by his own reckoning), could not give.

This is a great example of what I call Type B prophetic evangelism. To summarise the difference between the two approaches, Type A involves God speaking to a believer about an unbeliever:

God $\Longrightarrow$ Believer $\Longrightarrow$ Unbeliever

This is 'mediated revelation' (i.e. revelation given through a human intermediary). Type B is 'immediate revelation'. In other words, it is revelation given directly by God to an unbeliever, without a human intermediary:

God $\Longrightarrow$ Unbeliever

In the light of all this, I now want to propose two things. Firstly, that both types of prophetic evangelism are entirely biblical. Secondly, that both are being found more and more today.

Prophetic Evangelism in the Old Testament

It may be a surprise to learn that prophecy was used to bring pagan people to a knowledge of God in Old Testament times. Joseph employed 'dream interpretation' in his witness to Pharaoh. Elijah and Elisha both used prophecy in their witness to pagans. But perhaps the pre-eminent prophetic evangelist in the Old Testament is Daniel. In the book of Daniel, chapters 1–4, Daniel, the prophet, and Nebuchadnezzar, the pagan king of Babylon, both receive revelation. In other words, in these chapters of the Old Testament we see both Type A and Type B prophetic evangelism.

In the early passages of the book, Daniel is clearly described as being endowed with the ability to have visions and interpret prophetic phenomena. In Daniel 1:17 we read, 'Daniel could understand visions and dreams of all kinds' (NIV).

One night King Nebuchadnezzar had a dream that greatly troubled him. He asked his court magicians, sorcerers, astrologers and enchanters to come and interpret it. They failed – not that they had much of a chance, given that the king refused to tell them what the dream actually was. The king, furious, sent out an order for all the wise men in his kingdom to be executed. When the arresting officer arrived to kill Daniel and his companions, the prophet asked for more time, saying that he would tell the king what his dream was and what it meant. We then read in 2:19 that 'during the night the mystery was revealed to Daniel in a vision' (NIV).

Daniel told the arresting officer not to kill the wise men of the kingdom but asked him instead to take him to the king. Daniel came before the king and witnessed to him, saying, 'No wise man, enchanter, magician or diviner can explain to the king the mystery he has asked about, but there is a God in heaven who reveals mysteries' (2:27–28, NIV).

Daniel then repeated the king's dream and explained that every detail was prophetic concerning future events. The scene concluded with the pagan king honouring God:

> *Then King Nebuchadnezzar fell prostrate before Daniel and paid him honour and ordered that an offering and incense be presented to him. The king said to Daniel, 'Surely your God is the God of gods and the Lord of kings and a revealer of mysteries, for you were able to reveal this mystery' (Dan. 2:46–47, NIV).*

In these first two chapters of the book of Daniel we see Daniel using prophetic revelation to interpret a pagan king's dreams, with the result that this unbeliever acknowledges that Daniel's God is King. In other words, both types of prophetic evangelism occur in Daniel 1–2: Types A and B. Indeed, both types occur in Daniel 3–4. Eventually the king proclaims:

> *It is my pleasure to tell you about the miraculous signs and wonders that the Most High God has performed for me. How great are his signs, how mighty his wonders! His kingdom is an eternal kingdom; his dominion endures from generation to generation (Dan. 4:2–3, NIV).*

What is powerfully evident from these words is that prophecy, used in evangelism, clearly comes into the category of the miraculous. It is a powerful witness to those who don't know God. Even in the time of Daniel God was saying, 'Prophecy is a potent tool in evangelism!'

Here then, in the Old Testament era, we see prophetic phenomena being used to bring a pagan ruler to the point of repenting of his sins and acknowledging Israel's God to be the one who saves.

There is Type A in that Daniel receives prophetic insight about the meaning of an unbeliever's dreams.

There is Type B in so far as King Nebuchadnezzar, a pagan king, is given dreams that are clearly divinely inspired.

Prophetic Evangelism in the New Testament

It should come as no surprise to hear that prophetic evangelism occurs frequently in the New Testament. When God poured out his Holy Spirit on the Day of Pentecost, two things among many occurred. First of all, the ability to prophesy was given to young and old, Jew and Gentile, rich and poor, men and women alike. Every believer, post-Pentecost, can now prophesy.

Secondly, every believer was given power to bear witness to Jesus. Jesus promised that his followers would receive power when the Holy Spirit came upon them and that they would be his witnesses in Jerusalem, Judea, Samaria and to the ends of the earth. In the years after Pentecost, the first Christians gradually took the Gospel out to the nations in the power of the Spirit. As they did this, prophetic evangelism was one of the methods used to convince unbelievers that the Gospel is true.

If you find this hard to believe, look at Simon Peter. Peter is filled with the Holy Spirit on the Day of Pentecost and he preaches the Gospel to the crowds. That he uses prophecy in his presentation may be indicated by two facts. First, when Peter is said to address the crowd in Acts 2:14 the word used is the one commonly used in the Greek version of the Old Testament for the declarations of the prophets. It was the word used for the prophets when they declared 'Thus says the Lord!' Luke (who wrote the book of Acts) is showing us that Peter's words come into the category of the prophetic.

Second, when Peter has finished his message and the listeners are deeply convicted, we are told that with many other words he encouraged his listeners to respond (Acts 2:40). The word translated 'encouraged' there (most translations use the word 'exhort') is from the same root as the word used for prophecy in 1 Corinthians 14:3: 'One who prophesies is helping others grow in the Lord, *encouraging* and comforting them'. Peter's first ministry task after Pentecost is to evangelise the crowds and he does so using the gift of prophecy. This leads to a great harvest – three thousand converted at the end of a single message! Again we should note the power of prophetic evangelism.

From this point on, Peter uses prophecy frequently in evangelising others. The most important example of this occurs in Acts 10, where we see both Type A and Type B of prophetic evangelism. A man called Cornelius receives a prophetic vision. He is not Jewish and he is not a Christian, but he is a seeker.

Then Peter receives a prophecy in the form of an open vision. In this vision he is given revelation about God's acceptance of 'unclean' Gentiles like Cornelius. This revelation comes to Peter as an enigmatic image.

As a result of these two prophecies, a divine appointment is established between the unbelievers (Cornelius and his household) and the believer (Peter), resulting in Peter preaching the Gospel and the unbelievers becoming followers of Christ. To put it another way, a Type B example of prophetic evangelism, followed by a Type A example, leads to a dramatic conversion of a number of Gentiles.

Type B: God Speaks Directly to Cornelius

Acts 10:1–8:

> *In Caesarea there lived a Roman army officer named Cornelius, who was a captain of the Italian Regiment. He was a devout man who feared the God of Israel, as did his entire household. He gave generously to charity and was a man who regularly prayed to God. One afternoon about three o'clock, he had a vision in which he saw an angel of God coming towards him. 'Cornelius!' the angel said. Cornelius stared at him in terror. 'What is it, sir?' he asked the angel. And the angel replied, 'Your prayers and gifts to the poor have not gone unnoticed by God! Now send some men down to Joppa to find a man named Simon Peter. He is staying with Simon, a leatherworker who lives near the shore. Ask him to come and visit you.' As soon as the angel was gone, Cornelius called two of his household servants and a devout soldier, one of his personal attendants. He told them what had happened and sent them off to Joppa.*

Type A: God Speaks to Peter about Cornelius

Acts 10:9–16:

> *The next day as Cornelius's messengers were nearing the city, Peter went up to the flat roof to pray. It was about midday, and he was hungry. But while lunch was being prepared, he fell into a trance. He saw the sky open, and something like a*

large sheet was let down by its four corners. In the sheet were all sorts of animals, reptiles, and birds. Then a voice said to him, 'Get up, Peter; kill and eat them.' 'Never, Lord,' Peter declared. 'I have never in all my life eaten anything forbidden by our Jewish laws.' The voice spoke again, 'If God says something is acceptable, don't say it isn't.' The same vision was repeated three times. Then the sheet was pulled up again to heaven.

As Cornelius and his household arrive at Peter's house, Peter understands the interpretation and the application of the vision. He realises that even though these people are non-Jews, God wants him to preach the Gospel to them. So he does, with great results!

Acts 10:44–46

Even as Peter was saying these things, the Holy Spirit fell upon all who had heard the message. The Jewish believers who came with Peter were amazed that the gift of the Holy Spirit had been poured out upon the Gentiles, too. And there could be no doubt about it, for they heard them speaking in tongues and praising God.

What Acts 10 shows us is the way in which God uses prophecy in evangelism. He uses prophetic phenomena in order to help those who are far away to come to acknowledge who he is. Indeed, we should really note that it is prophetic evangelism that causes the Gospel to break out of the confines of Jerusalem, Judea and Samaria to the ends of the earth. If we go back to the promise of Jesus in Acts 1:8, Jesus said that the Holy Spirit would come upon the disciples and that they would receive power to bear witness to him in ever-increasing circles of influence:

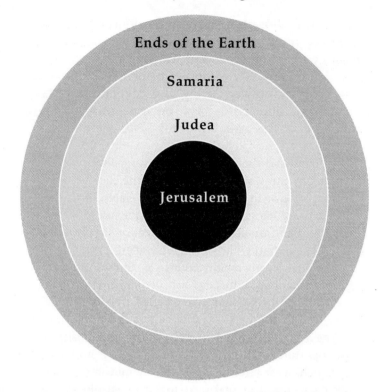

It is Peter's use of prophetic evangelism in Acts 10 that really begins the mission to non-Jews, or Gentiles, and makes possible the preaching of the Gospel to the ends of the earth.

Prophetic Evangelism Today: Type A

While prophetic evangelism has not commonly been in evidence during church history, it is certainly appearing more and more today.

Type A is definitely more in evidence. There are a significant number of Christian leaders who are using prophecy in evangelism, and teaching others to do the same. Here are a few examples of people I know who have recently started using the revelatory gifts in evangelism, and who have been running training conferences in this area. First, Steve Witt comments:

> Jesus modelled the revelatory for evangelism with the woman at the well (Jn. 4). After a brief, ice-breaking conversation with a woman drawing water, Jesus goes for the heart. He saw beyond the natural and spoke into her life. She immediately recognized a supernatural anointing and said, 'Sir, I perceive you are a prophet.'
>
> The effects were massive. Verse 39 states, 'And many of the Samaritans of that city believed in Him because of the word of the woman who testified, "He told me all that I ever did."'
>
> Feeling challenged, I have been watching and listening for opportunities. Recently I was on a flight from Vienna to Zurich, weary from a week of busy ministry. I found myself in an aisle seat next to a 64-year-old former Broadway singer. He was outgoing, and I knew this wouldn't be a quiet flight. As he talked, God began to help me see his life. I asked questions motivated by what I believed to be revelation knowledge. He quickly became intrigued by what seemed to him my unusual ability to see deeper than the given facts. Gradually he opened up more of his life and described the brokenness of divorce and rejection. I was no longer ministering to a stranger, but a new friend. As the pilot alerted us to prepare for landing I felt it was time for closure. I discussed the power of forgiveness and then I dropped the 'bomb': 'Would you mind if I pray with you?'

Without hesitation he folded his hands and bowed his head. I began what I call 'prophetically peppered prayer'. I prayed a normal prayer of blessing, but weaved into it things that only God would know. In short, I prayed beyond my own knowledge. As I finished, he was crying and grabbed my hand, saying, 'That's the most powerful prayer I've ever heard.' I handed him my card and went to my next gate.

Forty-five minutes later, while standing in a shop, I felt an abrupt tap on my shoulder. I turned to be greeted by my newfound friend panting from running to find me. He was ecstatic. He had been meditating on what was said and needed to thank me again. The card I had handed him said, 'Vineyard Christian Fellowship'. It turned out that years ago his grandparents grew a large vineyard in California. To him this was significant. He even thought it was 'spooky'. 'What a strange coincidence!' he exclaimed. Shaking his hand one last time I reassured him this was not a coincidence. I may not hear from this man again, but for a few moments we shared a taste of God's presence.

Another practitioner, **Doug Addison**, writes:

I was in Orlando this past weekend leading an outreach at the Florida Mall. Phil Zaldatte and I held a prophetic evangelism workshop on Friday. Then on Saturday afternoon we led a team of forty-five people into the mall for 'Holy Spirit divine encounters'.

I was totally stoked when my team approached our first table and asked if we could interpret a dream. They just happened to be talking about a dream and was wondering what it meant. We gave the woman the meaning and she was so touched and open that we led her to the Lord in front of her two friends.

Another team went out and took a 'prophetic stroll' down the mall. They walked around praying until the Lord spoke to them about a person. The Lord spoke to them to go and sit next to a guy who looked lonely. Within minutes he was revealing his feelings of emptiness and they prayed with him. Feeling a little more confident they moved to the next person that the Holy Spirit pointed out to them and he received the Lord after having a dream interpreted.

One particular group from our team had a sensation of 'hot tingling hands' as we started the event so I instructed them to look for sick people. They bee-lined to a lady with a withered hand and walking with a limp. All they had to say is that they felt God telling them to pray for her for healing in Jesus' name. As they prayed her withered hand opened and her foot straightened! She was so excited at the power of God that she received Jesus on the spot.

Our outreaches are normally low key and we don't see many salvations. We view evangelism as a process and we look for people who we can 'nudge' closer to God. To our surprise there were fourteen people who came to Jesus over the weekend! A handful of people who were not bold evangelists nervously took a walk down the mall and asked God to show them who needs a touch. Imagine what would happen if we got intentional and began trusting the Holy Spirit to guide us to people that need the Lord!

Prophetic Evangelism puts a new spin on reaching people with the love of God. We don't pass out tracts or Bibles but simply ask God for a specific word for someone and give it to them, or tell them the meaning of a dream. I believe that this type of outreach will be responsible for the 'renewal' of evangelism. Unlike the typical conference in which people sit and listen to a speaker (we did that too), the Lord wants to start using conferences to 'jump-start' people's gifts and display His power in the streets. We are noticing that each time we go out the power of God is increasing.

Steve Witt and Doug Addison are just two of a number of leaders I know who have been practising and teaching prophetic evangelism in recent years. In fact, it is very interesting to note how a number of us have, entirely independently of one another, been moved to teach about prophetic evangelism, to have a go ourselves and then to train the Body of Christ to try this approach at equipping conferences. Type A prophetic evangelism is certainly on the increase today.

Prophetic Evangelism Today: Type B

More and more unbelievers are receiving revelation from the Holy Spirit about Jesus. While some might argue that this does not qualify as prophecy, I disagree. In such instances, God is speaking! One of my favourite verses in the Bible at the moment is Isaiah 65:1:

> *The LORD says, 'People who never before inquired about me are now asking about me. I am being found by people who were not looking for me. To them I have said, "I am here!"'*

A thorough survey has been conducted of over six hundred ex-Muslims who now follow Jesus. The survey revealed that over a quarter of those interviewed confirmed that dreams and visions played a vital role in their conversion to Christianity.

A man from Guinea told of a person in white who

appeared to him in a dream, calling him with outstretched arms. This sort of dream, in which Christ appears as a figure in white, is a frequent pattern in missionary work among Muslims, according to the report.

A Muslim called Malay saw her dead Christian parents in a dream, celebrating in heaven. Jesus, in a white robe, told her, 'If you want to come to me, come!' She realised that she had been trying to find God all her life and that God had now himself taken the initiative to reach her through Jesus.

According to the survey, some of the dreams experienced by Muslims have involved the following:

'Two angels in white clothes were standing on the summit of a mountain. Jesus was standing between the angels, and as I knelt, he laid his hands on my head . . .'

'I dreamt that I was sitting on a chair with my arms bound. Then a man came, who I recognised as Jesus, and touched the bonds, which fell away from me . . .'

'In my dream, Jesus told me to come to him and read the Bible. He would show me the way, the truth and the life . . .'

'I saw Christians waiting in a line leading towards heaven. I tried to join the line, but a very large being blocked my path. I started to cry, because the side I was standing on was truly awful, but the place where the others were standing was unbelievably beautiful . . .'

A missionary working among the Tausugs, the Philippines' largest Muslim people group, reports that a number of faithful Muslims 'saw Jesus' in their dreams following Ramadan in 2003.

One man could hardly believe it when he dreamed of Jesus killing a huge dragon in a duel. The following day, he had the same dream again, and became open to hear the Gospel.

A member of the Yakan people in Basilan Province

dreamed the prophet Muhammad could not look Jesus in the eye. When he told his cousin, a Christian, of the dream, his cousin told him that the dream meant that Jesus is greater than Muhammad.

This research reveals what many of us are encountering in actual experience: that people who don't know Jesus are receiving prophetic revelation by the Holy Spirit. This is certainly happening to Muslims. It is happening to people of other faiths and of no faith. It is happening in the East and it is beginning to happen more and more in the West.

None of this should surprise us. Experiences of God are widespread even in the UK. In support of this claim we need look no further than the Alister Hardy Research Centre in Manchester. This was set up to 'make a disciplined study of the frequency of report of firsthand religious or transcendent experience . . . and to investigate the nature and function of that experience'. A poll conducted in 1985 suggested that fifteen million Britons would say that at least once or twice in their lives they have been aware of, or have been influenced by, a presence or power. A further survey in 1986 suggested that nearly half of the UK population has had a transcendental experience, with nearly 80 per cent of people claiming this was an experience of God. Of these positive respondents over half never attended a place of worship and many have never told anyone of their experiences.

So we should not be surprised by the fact that non-religious people are having religious experiences. What is surprising, and indeed revealing, is the fact that Muslims are having revelations of Jesus. One of the arguments used by atheists to counter the spiritual nature of these experiences is that research often shows Hindus having Hindu experiences, Muslims having Muslim experiences, and so on. In other words, atheistic scientists argue that such experiences are culturally conditioned. If that is so, how do we explain Muslims having visions of Jesus Christ? This is hardly conditioned by culture!

The only conclusion that makes sense is that the dreams and visions about Jesus being currently experienced by people of other faiths and no faith are examples of genuine prophecy. If this is the case, the church needs to wake up to what the Holy Spirit is doing, not just in the church but outside the church too.

The Gospel is the Main Thing

In this book I will attempt to show how powerful prophecy can be in witnessing to lost people. In doing this, however, I want to be very clear about one thing. Our focus should not be on prophecy itself. Prophetic revelation is just a means to an end. The end is the proclamation of the Gospel. It is the Gospel, not the gift, that should be the focus of our attention.

Revelatory phenomena have a power to fascinate people for their own sake. When that happens, prophecy can so easily become the focus of a Christian's or a church's mission. But gifts like prophecy should never be the centre of our priorities. The Gospel is the central priority. Gifts like prophecy revolve around that one fixed centre. They exist to serve the proclamation of the Good News that Jesus died for our sins on the Cross.

One example of prophetic evangelism in the New Testament is in Acts 8:26–40, where Philip witnesses to an Ethiopian eunuch. Every step of the way, Philip is directed by the prophetic voice of God. He is told where to go and he is told what to do. All this in relation to a seeker! What could be a clearer illustration of prophetic evangelism than this?

Yet when Philip has got the man's attention, it is not the prophetic revelations he has been receiving that he talks about, it is the message of Jesus Christ. The seeker has been reading the great prophecy of Calvary in Isaiah 53. Philip uses this as the basis for sharing the Gospel. As Luke records in Acts 8:35, 'So Philip began with this same Scripture and then used many others to tell him the Good News about Jesus.'

I would very much like to encourage all of us to listen to what the Father is saying with greater attentiveness in our relationships with those who don't as yet know Jesus. At the same time, I would also like to encourage us to use this gift as a means of helping unbelievers to see and to know that the same Jesus who died on the Cross and who rose again is very real and relevant to everyone today. If prophetic revelation can help us get to that point – to the point where the lost confess that Jesus is Lord – then we cannot go far wrong.

Chapter 2

JUST ONE OF MANY METHODS

One of the verses that I have been led to meditate on recently is 2 Samuel 14:14:

Like water spilled on the ground, which cannot be recovered, so we must die. But God does not take away life; instead, he devises ways so that a lost person [literally 'a banished person'] may not remain estranged from him (NIV).

In these powerful words we are reminded once again of our mortality, of the inevitable fact that we will all one day die. But these same words teach us that God is not in the business of destroying us but rather coming up with different ways of bringing the *nadach* (Hebrew), those abandoned and lost, back to himself. The ways he chooses are, in the original sense of the word, 'cunning'. God has come up with subtle ways of bringing death-bound human beings back into a saving relationship with himself. He knows that we easily resist his advances because of our sinful desire to manage our lives on our own. So his ways are subtle. He does not use just one very obvious way of appealing to our stubborn hearts. Rather, he has decided on many and clever ways.

All this has huge implications for evangelism. God has provided *one way* of salvation, through the finished work of Christ on the Cross. At the same time, he has devised different and creative methods of drawing people to the Cross, there to get right with himself. In this chapter I want to look at prophetic evangelism but I want to do so in the context of other methods. So we will look at the following as a sample list of God's methods:

Programmed evangelism
Presence evangelism
Proclamation evangelism
Persuasion evangelism
Prayer evangelism
Power evangelism
Prophetic evangelism

Method 1: Programmed Evangelism

I pray that you may be active in sharing your faith, so that you will have a full understanding of every good thing we have in Christ (Philemon. 6).

Those who fail to plan, plan to fail: so the saying goes. Programmed evangelism simply means having an intentional strategy to witness to seekers, whether as an individual or as a church.

Many churches fail to plan ways to reach their community with the Father's love. They should therefore not be surprised when they fail. God expects us to strategise ways of witnessing to our locality and beyond. Too many people today are praying for revival and doing nothing in the meantime. What they really want is God to come and do their evangelism for them!

So God calls us to be *active*, not passive, in sharing our faith. He calls us to think and pray about ways we can reach out in his love and power to the people in our family, our neighbourhood, our workplace – in the networks of our significant relationships with the unchurched.

One of the most encouraging examples of programmed evangelism I've heard recently came in a letter from a woman called Stephanie. She had brought her unbelieving husband to our church about four years ago when J. John and I were doing a series of guest services at St Andrew's on the Ten Commandments. She brought her husband to the meeting on 'You shall not steal'. J. John finished the message on that subject and asked those who wanted to give their lives to Christ to put up their hands. Stephanie's husband gave his life to Jesus that night and he and his wife started to relate to Jesus as a couple. Needless to say, Stephanie was overjoyed!

Last year they started planning an outreach for their neighbourhood for Christmas. They decided to invite everyone on their street to an evening of drinks and food at their house. They invited over fifty households. In the event about thirty came and they put up an awning in the back of their house to make room for everyone. Those who came loved the experience and those who didn't were very apologetic they couldn't come. The only negative comments they had were from two households on their streets, both occupied by Christians who said 'It'll never work.'

Well, it *did* work. The next day all the people who had come to the party were waving to each other as they went to work. People in the neighbourhood knew each other's names. One household (not Christian) decided to start planning for a big neighbourhood summer barbecue. Stephanie and her husband started preparing for the following Christmas get-together!

I find this sort of thing inspiring. Here are a couple who became Christians and who wanted to reach out to their neighbours. They thought and prayed about what they should do and started with the idea of a Christmas party. They planned for that and it worked. It worked so well that the neighbourhood is buzzing and those who didn't come were provoked to jealousy! Most important of all, it silenced the complaining of those who said 'It can't be done'! Nothing is ever achieved by people who say that. As the poem goes:

> *The one who misses all the fun*
> *Is he who says, 'It can't be done'.*
> *In solemn pride, he stands aloof*
> *And greets each venture with reproof.*
> *Had he the power, he would efface*
> *The history of the human race.*
> *We'd have no radio, no cars,*
> *No streets lit by electric stars,*
> *No telegraph, no telephone,*
> *We'd linger in the age of stone.*
> *The world would sleep if things were run*
> *By folks who say, 'It can't be done'.*

Method 2: Presence Evangelism

> *Live such good lives among the pagans that, though they accuse you of doing wrong, they may see your good deeds and glorify God on the day he visits us (1 Pet. 2:12, NIV).*

Presence evangelism simply means being a positive presence among those who do not know Jesus Christ. Whether in the neighbourhood or in the work place, it means being salt and light. It means in essence being a good example – an example pointing to Jesus Christ.

The number one way of being a good witness is through serving the needs of others. For this reason what I am here calling 'presence evangelism' is sometimes referred to as 'servant evangelism'. In this context, St Francis of Assisi is often quoted: 'Go throughout the world preaching the Gospel, and use words if you have to.'

According to the book *Life of Francis of Assisi*, Francis once invited a young monk to join him on a trip to town to preach. Honoured to be given the invitation, the monk readily accepted. All day long he and Francis walked through the streets, byways and alleys, and even into the suburbs. They rubbed shoulders with hundreds of people. At day's end, the two headed back home. Not even once had Francis addressed a crowd, nor had he talked to anyone about the Gospel. Greatly disappointed, his young companion said, 'I thought we were going into town to preach.' Francis responded, 'My son, we have preached. We were preaching while we were walking. We were seen by many and our behaviour was closely watched. It is of no use to walk anywhere to preach unless we preach everywhere as we walk!'

Presence evangelism is a very powerful resource. Not long ago I was in prayer for my church at St Andrew's. As I started to pray, the Lord gave me a picture. It was of the main street of my town. Everywhere I looked I could see people in sunglasses. The very elderly were wearing shades. So were the very young and everyone in between. Even babies in prams had sunglasses on.

As I looked, I felt led to ask one of the people why everyone was wearing shades. In response they pointed up towards the hill where St Andrew's Church is situated. They said, 'because of the light pouring out of that church'. As soon as they said that, I was reminded of these words of the Lord Jesus in Matthew 5:

You are the light of the world – like a city on a mountain, glowing in the night for all to see. Don't hide your light under a basket! Instead, put it on a stand and let it shine for all. In the same way, let your good deeds shine out for all to see, so that everyone will praise your heavenly Father (Mt. 5:14–16).

Many years ago some men were panning for gold in Montana, and one of them found an unusual stone. Breaking it open, he was excited to see that it contained gold. Working eagerly, the men soon discovered an abundance of the precious metal. Happily, they began shouting with delight, 'We've found it! We've found gold! We're rich!' They had to interrupt their celebrating, though, to go into a nearby town and stock up on supplies. Before they left camp, the men agreed not to tell a soul about their find. Indeed, no one breathed a word about it to anyone while they were in town. Much to their dismay, however, when they were about to return, hundreds of men were prepared to follow them. When they asked the crowd to tell who had 'squealed', the reply came, 'No one had to. Your faces showed it!'

I really believe it is God's will for the local church to make an impact on its community by being a positive presence. At its best, the local church shines with the light of Jesus and brings glory to the Father.

Method 3: Proclamation Evangelism

And then he told them, 'Go into all the world and preach the Good News to everyone, everywhere' (Mk. 16:15).

People often quote St Francis' motto about using words only if you have to as a great way of excusing them from

opening their mouths in evangelism! As my good friend
J. John often says, 'Most Christians are like Arctic rivers:
they are frozen at the mouth.' St Francis never meant his
proverb to be used as a reason for *not* speaking to people
about Jesus, only to underline that a person whose
lifestyle is bad news has no right to verbalise good news!
We have to *be* good news among the lost before we have
the right to *share* good news.

Assuming we are good news, we must actually *talk*
about Jesus to those who do not know him.

Recently we had a painter around our house. He was
with us for about ten days on and off, repainting the
vicarage. On his last day, after having made him coffee, I
decided this was the moment to talk to him properly. It
was in fact he who started the conversation. He began by
saying the car park of our church was always full, and
how amazed he was by the hundreds of people who use
our church in the week. He then started talking about his
experiences of church. He had been made to go as a child
but – as with so many in the UK – had rebelled as a
teenager and never gone back. This started a further litany
of woes about the church. At this point I stopped him.

'You're talking about one of my least favourite
subjects.'

'What's that?' he asked

'The church.'

'But you're a vicar! It should be your *favourite* subject!'

'No, it's my least favourite subject because everyone
has their horror stories about church, including me. It's
not the church I'm interested in.'

'Well, what *are* you interested in?'

'I'm interested in Jesus . . .'

'Yes, so am I, actually. He was a really good man . . .'

'Yes, *amazing* . . .'

There then followed an exchange of views about Jesus in which I shared why I think Jesus is such Good News for us today. Even though the church may often feel like *bad* news, Jesus is *good* news.

I could see the man being moved as I spoke, so I decided to finish the conversation on a high by telling him the following joke:

'Have you ever heard about the painter who had a dramatic conversion to Christianity?'

'No,' my friend replied.

'He woke up in the night and heard God say to him in a loud voice, *"Repaint and thin no more!"'*

The man I was speaking to was quiet for a moment and looked at me quizzically. He then started to roar with laughter. I went indoors and heard him round the back of the house telling his mate what I had said about Jesus and the church, then repeating my rather feeble joke. His mate then fell about laughing too. I had a chuckle as well, as I realised that one unsaved painter was unwittingly evangelising his mate using humour!

I quote this recent incident not to paint myself in any great light (forgive the pun) but to show what fun it can be to actually verbalise the Good News about Jesus. All we have to do is be normal, be relevant, and be interesting. We need to open our mouths and talk about Jesus in an enthusiastic way. Sadly most believers have applied Jesus' command in the Gospels to themselves: 'Tell no one!'

And one more thing – we don't need to say too much! It's always good to quit while you're winning! Someone else can take on the baton at a later time, leading that person further on in the journey towards salvation. Our job is to be faithful in the little part we have in saying what God puts it in our heart to say.

Method 4: Persuasion Evangelism

> *Always be prepared to give an answer to everyone who asks*
> *you to give the reason for the hope that you have. But do this*
> *with gentleness and respect . . . (1 Pet. 3:15, NIV).*

Not long ago my family and I had to go to my mother's
80th birthday party in an exclusive London club. We
were not greatly looking forward to the prospect because
we do not cope very well with formal occasions. On the
morning in question I woke up with a strong sense that
the Lord was saying that I was to put on the shoes of the
readiness to share the Gospel of peace. So, before I
dressed, I prayed on the armour of God (Eph. 6:10ff) and
made a big deal of saying to the Lord, 'I'm ready to share
the Gospel today.' Instead of a sense of reluctance, I was
filled with a sense of excitement.

When we arrived I was greeted by my uncle – an
eminent medic, and a vocal atheist. I knew straight away
that the day was not going to be boring! As we were
seated at the beautifully furnished dining table, guess
who I was sitting next to. Yes, my atheistic uncle.
Everything went fine until we got to the point between
the main course and the dessert. My uncle decided –
while there was a lull in the general conversation – to
start having a very loud go at me for believing in God.
He was extremely outspoken and dogmatic about his
views.

As I sat there, I noticed that my four children were
looking at me nervously. They were thinking, 'What's
Dad going to say here?' Even the waiters and waitresses
stopped to listen in on the conversation, eagerly awaiting
the outcome.

I started to pray quietly and as I did so the peace of

God came upon me. I addressed my uncle – who is not slim, and who likes his food – with these words:

'Were you hungry when you came to this dinner table today?'

'Yes, I certainly was. What's that got to do with it?'

'Well, you're the scientist, not me, but wouldn't you say that the existence of hunger in your life presupposes the existence of something that will satisfy that hunger – namely food?'

'Of course,' said my uncle.

'Well, the fact is, there are millions and millions of people today who are spiritually hungry. They are hungry for something that money, a good home, and even relationships, cannot satisfy.'

'Yes, so what?'

'Well, you have just told me that the existence of a physical hunger in our lives presupposes the existence of food – something that satisfies that hunger.'

'Yes . . .'

'I would like to suggest that the existence of spiritual hunger all over the world – shared even by people in this room – presupposes the existence of something or, better still, Some One who can satisfy that spiritual hunger.'

'Oh. I've never thought about it that way before. . . .'

'Yes, and that spiritual hunger *can* be satisfied, Uncle, just like your physical hunger has been satisfied by this great food.'

Then I paused before concluding thus:

'You know that my football team is Norwich City and that the chairman is a committed Christian and a great cook, Delia Smith.'

'Yes.'

'Well, she said: "Taste the goodness of the Lord that

alone satisfies the deepest longings of the soul." You need to taste and see that the Lord is good.'

My uncle was quiet for the rest of the meal.

Now what was going on here? I would like to propose that this was an example of 'persuasion' evangelism. In the Scripture passage above, 1 Peter 3:15, the apostle encourages us to be ever-ready, always prepared, to give an intelligent defence of what we believe and hope for.

In order to do this (and we are told to do it with gentleness and respect), we must know some theology. We cannot simply expect to give good answers to tough questions if we haven't done some study and research ourselves. Talking with non-Christians about Christianity is a great way of showing how much we do know and how much we don't know! It challenges and excites us not only to *do* the stuff but also to *know* our stuff!

Persuasion evangelism – sometimes called 'apologetics' – is going to be a very important way of reaching the unchurched in the future. For this reason, every year I teach a course on basic Christian doctrine. It runs over ten sessions and it is based on the challenge of 1 Peter 3:15. In other words, it is a course of basic Bible theology that is designed to help believers answer the tough questions that unbelievers ask. I do this because I am convinced that God wants us to grow in wisdom as well as power. Jesus Christ is both the Wisdom of God and the Power of God. We need both if we are to be effective in reaching a lost world.

So, here is a list of the topics:

Can we Trust the Bible? (Doctrine of Scripture)
Does God Really Exist? (Doctrine of God)
Whose World is it Anyway? (Doctrine of Creation)
What is God Like? (Doctrine of the Trinity)

Is my Future Fixed? (Doctrine of Predestination)
Why do Human Beings Suffer? (Doctrine of Evil)
What's so Different about Jesus? (Doctrine of Christ)
Why was the Cross Necessary? (Doctrine of the Cross)
Why do I Need the Holy Spirit? (Doctrine of the Spirit)
Where is History Heading? (Doctrine of Eschatology)

You can order the tapes of these talks from the address at the end of this book. That way you too can be equipped to be more effective at 'persuasion evangelism'. Ultimately, of course, it is the Holy Spirit who does the persuading. It is he alone who convicts the sinner and reveals Jesus to the unbeliever's seeking heart. At the same time, we can cooperate with the Holy Spirit by being wiser in our presentation of God's truth.

Method 5: Prayer Evangelism

When you enter a house, first say, 'Peace to this house.' If a man of peace is there, your peace will rest on him; if not, it will return to you (Lk. 10:5–6, NIV).

Another translation of these same verses reads as follows:

Whenever you enter a home, give it your blessing. If it is worthy of the blessing, the blessing will stand; if not, the blessing will return to you (The Living Bible).

Ed Silvoso has been greatly used by the Lord in Argentina, as well as in the UK and in Europe, where he has shared some of the insights he has learned first-hand in the Argentinian revival. One of the things Ed has been teaching is about 'prayer evangelism'. This takes a number of forms, but chief among them is the untapped power of asking God to bless those who don't know him. Indeed, Ed often stresses the importance of talking to God about our neighbours before talking to our neighbours about God. In our talking to God, Ed encourages us to speak blessings over those who don't know Christ.

I'll never forget how, at a conference for four hundred young evangelists, Ed told the following story of an outreach team in Buenos Aires. They had just taken a break for lunch and were sitting in a restaurant. The waitress brought some fish for their main meal and they decided to give thanks and bless it. One of the team shared that he thought this was not the best idea, that instead of blessing a dead fish they should bless something living. So they turned to the waitress and said, 'We're Christians and we believe God wants to bless you. Is there anything we can ask God to bless you with?'

The young woman thought for a moment and then said, 'I really need transport in my work. There is a little black Fiat that's for sale and would be ideal but I just don't know if I could afford it. You could ask God to help me with that.'

'Sure thing,' said the team leader and they asked her to close her eyes while they prayed.

Barely had he got through the prayer when they all noticed that she was crying. They tried to comfort her but she told them, 'I'm crying not because I'm upset but because no one has ever cared enough about me to ask God to bless me.'

That woman gave her life to Christ, as did six other members of staff at the restaurant.

Prayer evangelism is a proven, useful tool for reaching out to the lost with the power of God's love. I know for a fact that Ed Silvoso's pioneering ministry in this area has borne fruit, and not just in Argentina. He and I both speak and minister in a city in Norway where this way of evangelising has proved effective. Indeed, many believers from different streams have united to bless their city in prayer. This includes taking very seriously 1 Timothy 2:1–4, where Paul writes:

> *I urge you, first of all, to pray for all people. As you make your requests, plead for God's mercy upon them, and give thanks. Pray this way for kings and all others who are in authority, so that we can live in peace and quietness, in godliness and dignity. This is good and pleases God our Saviour, for he wants everyone to be saved and to understand the truth.*

There is no doubt that the whole spiritual atmosphere in that place is changing as different churches unite in prayer and ask God's blessing on their community. So prayer evangelism is another powerful means of outreach.

Method 6: Power Evangelism

> *Go and announce to them that the Kingdom of Heaven is near. Heal the sick, raise the dead, cure those with leprosy, and cast out demons. Give as freely as you have received! (Mt. 10:7–8).*

It was John Wimber who introduced the concept of 'power evangelism' to me back in the early 1980s. His teaching focused on the Kingdom of God, the central theme in the teaching of Jesus. Wimber reminded us that Jesus' teaching on the Kingdom of God came not only with words but also with works. God's dynamic rule was proclaimed in Jesus' message and it was demonstrated in his miracles. John Wimber encouraged the churches to believe that God's power was still available today and that we can evangelise people more effectively when the lost see signs, wonders and miracles.

It is this emphasis on the miracles that accredit and accompany the message that accounts for the word 'power' in the phrase 'power evangelism'. Wimber showed how important it is today to evangelise in the way that Jesus did. This means not only giving a verbal testimony but also daring to pray for demonstrations of power in evangelism.

As an example, this is what a member of my church called Mike reported to me:

I work as a banker in the City of London. Following a recent conference my department of about thirty people organised a social evening in a local pub. During the course of the evening I became aware of a middle-aged woman, well dressed, but clearly suffering from either a mental illness or alcoholism. She was becoming increasingly incoherent and annoying to everyone in the pub. Eventually the bar manager decided to ask her to leave.

At this stage she became violent, slapping the bar manager and wrestling a large, well-built South African barman to the floor. She then ran to a corner of the pub and started to throw empty beer bottles and glasses in all directions.

Either through stupidity or divine conviction I approached the woman and once I was within a few feet of her I simply asked, 'What is your name?' She immediately calmed down but did not answer. I then asked her three times but received no response except a stare. I then said, 'In the name of Jesus, be healed and be gone.'

At this she stared at me with black eyes that I remember seemed full of both anger and pain. She then literally turned round and sprinted from the pub.

Sad that I could not do anything for her, I turned round, only to see my entire department, and the bar staff, staring at me. Then they asked, almost in unison, 'What did you say to her?'

The episode has been a good witness to the power of Jesus to my work colleagues and I know that I can now say that I have seen demons flee at the name of Jesus.

Method 7: Prophetic Evangelism

Let love be your highest goal, but also desire the special abilities the Spirit gives, especially the gift of prophecy (1 Cor. 14:1).

Paul encourages all believers to desire charismatic gifts, and he singles out prophecy as the one gift he thinks everyone should put first on their list. As far as the fruit of the Spirit is concerned, everyone should pursue love first. As far as the gifts of the Spirit are concerned, everyone should pursue the prophetic first. Indeed, the word translated 'desire' can also be rendered 'covet'. We are to be greedy for the gift of prophecy.

A few verses later Paul makes it very clear that the gift of prophecy is not just meant to comfort those who already know Christ (verse 3), it is also designed to convict those who don't. So in verses 24–25 he writes about how the gift of prophecy can radically impact the lives of unbelievers:

If all of you are prophesying, and unbelievers or people who don't understand these things come into your meeting, they will be convicted of sin, and they will be condemned by what you say. As they listen, their secret thoughts will be laid bare, and they will fall down on their knees and worship God, declaring, 'God is really here among you.'

Here we see in the clearest terms that one of the reasons we are to desire the gift of prophecy is so that we can be more effective in evangelism. As we prophesy, unbelievers who are listening experience profound conviction as the secrets of their hearts are exposed. These secrets, as we will see later, need not necessarily be secret sins. They could also be secret hurts or wounds. Whatever the case, the use of prophecy in evangelism brings these things to the surface and causes unbelievers to recognise that God is alive.

As an example, let me describe something that happened a couple of years ago. We were coming to the end of a family service at St Andrew's. These are usually packed with young families, with many children present. On the Sunday morning in question, the family service team had decided to do a presentation of the parable of the prodigal son in Luke 15. Only, instead of portraying the father as forgiving and welcoming, they decided to do an ironic reversal and portray him as unforgiving and unwelcoming. So when the prodigal son returned they presented the father saying, 'What are you doing coming back like this? Go back to where you've come from. You're not welcome here!' Then, in the concluding part of the service, the team re-presented the parable showing the father as he really is in the story, lavishly and extravagantly merciful.

As the team leader asked me to come and give the

blessing, I sensed a very strong impression that the presentation had powerfully impacted someone in the church. I spoke out the following words that just dropped into my heart quite suddenly:

'There is someone here today who has been living with a deep sense of fatherlessness. You have been looking for your father all your life. Recently you have found him but you were really disappointed. Today, hearing about God the Father, you have realised that this is the Dad you've been looking for, and the Lord is saying to you, "It's time to come home."'

After the service people came forward for prayer. One of the people was a middle-aged lady called Mandy, not a Christian. She had been abandoned by her dad as a young girl and had been looking for him all her life. Recently she had discovered that he was in the Navy and had gone to meet him, but had felt bitterly rejected. That morning God had indeed been speaking to her about what a loving Father he is. She was powerfully impacted by the prophetic word uttered before the blessing and gave her life to the Lord Jesus Christ. That morning the 'father-shaped hole' in her heart was filled by the power of God's love as she received forgiveness and was filled with the Holy Spirit.

This, then, is how prophetic evangelism works. The most typical expression is like the above. A believer receives a strong impression, a sensation, a picture or even a vision concerning someone who doesn't know God. When revelation like this comes, the one receiving it just knows that they have to share it. The key is to do that sensitively and clearly. Once that has happened, then most often the person just has to trust the Lord that the word will bear fruit. It is not always the case that you find out just how life-changing the word actually was.

This kind of prophetic evangelism can happen in a public meeting in church or in a private meeting with an individual. 1 Corinthians 14:20–25 – the passage we have just looked at – shows how it can be used in public worship. But it is equally effective in private witnessing, as we will see in the rest of this book.

By All Means Saving Some

How often does this sort of thing happen? Or, to put it another way, how often is this sort of thing *supposed* to happen?

As far as public worship is concerned, 1 Corinthians 14:24–25 suggests to me that it is not supposed to be rare. Prophecy is supposed to be a regular feature of our corporate worship and it is meant to have at least some impact beyond just those who are Christians.

The same goes for one-to-one evangelism. When we have an opportunity to share our faith with a non-Christian, I believe the evidence of the New Testament is that we are meant to be listening to what the Father is saying about the person concerned. As John Wimber reminded us, the hallmark of Jesus' ministry is that he only ever did what he saw the Father doing and he only ever said what he heard the Father saying. Many of us follow the WWJD principle: 'What Would Jesus Do?' Jesus did a lot of prophetic evangelism. I think he expects us to as well.

God has devised many ways of bringing lost people back into relationship with himself, as we saw at the start of this chapter. Prophetic evangelism is just one method among others. As we will see, it is a particularly potent method today. But it is still just one method. Not all believers will feel attracted to it or comfortable with it.

Indeed, out of the seven methods above, prophetic evangelism may not be the one you relate to most. Having said that, I do believe that this approach is something that the Holy Spirit is encouraging many more people to have a go at.

At the same time, prophetic evangelism is not the only means by which someone is going to come to know the Lord. In reality, the typical seeker probably needs up to ten or more positive experiences of Christianity before deciding whether or not to follow the Lord Jesus Christ. In the process of having these positive experiences, the seeker concerned may well be exposed to a whole range of different methods of evangelism.

In this respect, I think of one of my next-door neighbours. She has recently given her life to Christ. Her journey towards Jesus involved being on the receiving end of the following:

- Programmed evangelism (through being invited to a Christmas party planned well in advance by believers on her street)
- Presence evangelism (being cared for in practical ways by neighbourly Christians)
- Proclamation evangelism (being invited to, and attending, an Alpha course and hearing the Gospel)
- Power evangelism (being exposed to the power of God at a midweek healing meeting, where she eventually gave her life to Christ)

God has devised many clever ways of bringing lost people back to himself. Prophetic evangelism is just one of many ways. But it is still a very important way, especially in the twenty-first century. As Paul wrote in 1 Corinthians 9:22–23:

Yes, I try to find common ground with everyone so that I might bring them to Christ. I do all this to spread the Good News, and in doing so I enjoy its blessings.

The NIV renders these verses as follows:

I have become all things to all men so that by all possible means I might save some. I do all this for the sake of the gospel, that I may share in its blessings.

Prophetic evangelism is one of the means we have at our disposal. Just how important it is we will see in the next chapter.

Chapter 3

A GREAT RESOURCE
FOR THE HARVEST

About seven years ago I was sitting in the vestry of a church in the east end of Oslo in Norway. I had just finished preaching and ministering at a conference in the church there and I was relaxing. As I sat down and rested, I had the strongest sense that the Holy Spirit was speaking to me out of the incident involving Jesus and the Samaritan woman in John chapter 4.

This passage is one I had preached on many times. Back in 1995 I had spoken at a conference in Derby and spent four whole sessions just going through this one episode reported in verses 4–42. I really didn't think there was very much else to glean from this passage. But I was wrong.

The Woman With No Name

John 4:4–42 is a great quarry for those who want to dig for gems about witnessing. The story starts with Jesus returning to Galilee from Judea. He feels compelled to go via Samaria and finds himself tired and thirsty by Jacob's well. It is noon and the sun is shining at its most intense. Consequently, no one else is present. Who in their right mind would come to draw water at the hottest time of the day?

Just then a woman approaches. She has her heavy

stone water jar with her. She is balancing it expertly on her head, as she has done so many times. Her face is red from the exertion and beads of sweat are glowing on her forehead. She sees Jesus and eyes him suspiciously. She can see clearly from his hair, his skin colour and his clothing that he is a Jewish man. Not only that, but his prayer shawl tells her that he is a rabbi. Her hackles rise.

As she prepares to lower her jar into the still, deep water of the well, Jesus looks at her and says, 'Please would you give me a drink?' At this she winces. She is deeply shocked. He is a Jew. She is a Samaritan. He is a man. She is a woman. This Jewish rabbi is not supposed to talk to a woman he doesn't know in public. What does he think he's doing?

She firmly points out that he is breaking the rules, the social conventions of the day, and asks him why he has requested a drink. At this point Jesus replies, 'If only you knew the gift God has for you and who it is you are talking to, you would be asking *me* for a drink, and I would give you living water.'

The woman, taking him literally, replies sarcastically that he hasn't got either a rope or a bucket. Since the well is very deep, there is no chance of him providing this 'living water'. And in any case, it is hard to imagine anyone greater than Jacob, the patriarch who gave the well to the Samaritans. Is this man claiming to be greater than Jacob? Is he telling her that he can give something even greater than the water Jacob supplied?

'This water,' says Jesus, 'is indeed inferior to what I am offering. After drinking this water, you'll soon be thirsty again. But the living water I have to offer will take away the thirst in your life for ever. The living water I give will become like an eternal fountain within your heart, supplying you with life that lasts for ever!'

At this the woman's heart is moved.

'Sir,' she cries. 'Give me some of this water. I want to drink so that my thirst disappears and I never have to visit this well again.'

'Go and fetch your husband,' Jesus replies.

There is an embarrassed silence.

'I don't have a husband,' the woman replies.

And now the key moment. Jesus, listening to what the Father is telling him about this woman, shares an insight into her life – an insight not learned by human means but by prophetic revelation. He says, 'That's true. You don't have a husband. You have been married to five husbands and the man you're currently living with isn't your husband.'

There is a pause as the woman recoils. Who could have told him that? Who has he been speaking to? Suddenly she sees it. He has not received this information by natural means. He is a prophet. He has seen the secrets of her heart. She is exposed. Her attempt to draw water at noon – when no one else is around – has failed. Her efforts to hide are of no avail.

'Sir,' she says, 'I see you are a prophet.'

As she realises that this man is a messenger from God, she begins to talk about religion. The prophetic revelation about her heart has suddenly made her open to talk about spiritual matters for the first time in ages. Jesus, realising that she has tried to fill the hole in her soul through relationships with men, points to the true Father in heaven. He says in effect, 'Don't look in men for what you can only truly find in the Perfect Father. He alone can satisfy the thirst for love that aches within your heart.' As he finishes, she tells him that the Messiah, when he eventually comes, will explain this kind of thing to her. Jesus replies, 'I, I am he.'

The woman drops her water jar and runs. She runs

and runs and runs. She is not running away from Jesus
out of fear. She is running to her town with a new
passion in her heart. 'Could it be? Could it be?' she asks
repeatedly under her breath. When she reaches town she
goes through the market place shouting, 'Come on!
Come on! Follow me to the well outside town. Come and
meet a man who knew everything about me without
anyone telling him a thing. Come and meet a man who
has read my deepest thoughts and seen my deepest
secrets. Could this be the Messiah?'

And as this nameless, faceless woman gasps and talks
all at the same time, a curiosity begins to rise up within
the inhabitants of this Samaritan community. All but a
few run out of their town, following the woman to the
well. Maybe the few who stayed behind were those who
would not fare very well if Jesus shared what he had seen
about the woman's secret wounds and sins. Whatever the
case, there is an astonishing spiritual harvest as scores of
non-Jews – hated Samaritans indeed – come to Jesus and
confess him as Saviour not just of Israel but of the world.

The woman's testimony has borne great fruit. Though
she has no name and will not be known until the end of
history, she has done well. As John writes:

> *Many Samaritans from the village believed in Jesus because the
> woman had said, 'He told me everything I ever did!' (Jn.4:39).*

The Power of a Prophetic Word

So what's the point? The point is this: as a result of one
prophetic revelation, a spiritual harvest occurred in the
most unlikely place. Jesus received an insight into this
woman's secret history and, as a result, she knew that

she was in the presence of one who could see her most hidden hurts and hang-ups. Far from making her flee in terror, Jesus' words about the Father woo her into a place of seeking after true love. This she receives and then gives away immediately to others. Indeed, her 'come and see' shows that she is an evangelist just like Philip in John 1:46, who also says 'come and see'.

And this is what happens when genuine prophetic revelation occurs. I often put it like this. Every person on the earth has a shadow. When they come into the sunlight, this shadow is exposed. Wherever they go, they cannot hide from this shadow, not while they are in the sun.

The same is true not just literally but figuratively. Each one of us has a spiritual shadow. It is the darkness of our inner life. It is the place where we hide the things that we feel guilty for and the things of which we feel most ashamed. It is the concealed space from which our sins, our wounds and our demons surface. It is the place we fear will be exposed.

It is this shadow that Jesus sees. He saw it in the people he met during his earthly ministry. He simply did not need any human information about the people he met. He knew everything about them by revelation. As John puts it in his Gospel: 'He did not need man's testimony about man, for he knew what was in a man' (Jn. 2:25, NIV).

And Jesus sees our shadows today. As the risen and exalted Lord, he looks with piercing eyes beneath the surface of our lives. As we read in Revelation 2:18, Jesus today has eyes that are brilliant with flames of fire. He announces himself in words that evoke holy fear: 'I am he who searches hearts and minds, and I will repay each of you according to your deeds' (Rev. 2:23, NIV). In the presence of the Son, our shadows are disclosed.

What is it that turns a woman from a sinner to a soul-winner in the matter of a few minutes in John 4? It is Jesus' use of the revelatory gift of prophecy. Yes, there are other factors too – for example, that he is prepared to relate to her cordially when cultural prejudice would say otherwise. The fact that he talks to her in a way that is relevant to her life is also critical (to a water-carrier he talks about water!). But the thing that catches her attention and indeed arrests her heart is that he sees prophetically 'everything I ever did'. This, along with the great news about intimacy with the Father, captivates her. Even though her shadow has been revealed, she knows she is in the presence of one who can truly rescue, heal and liberate her. This causes her to run into town, leaving her water jar behind.

Jesus never did get that drink!

Prophecy and the Word of Knowledge

What I sensed those years ago in Oslo was this: that God is going to release the gift of prophecy more and more to those who know and follow Jesus. This will be not only so that we can strengthen, encourage and comfort one another in the church, but also so that we can witness more powerfully and effectively to those who don't know Jesus. More than that, I sensed that God wants us to imitate Jesus in John 4 and to use prophetic evangelism in the coming harvest. In short, I sensed God saying that prophecy will be a great tool in the harvest.

But there is a barrier we need to overcome if we are to enter into the fullness of this destiny. This barrier is a barrier of misunderstanding, and it has to do with what in my opinion is a wrong understanding of what is called 'the word of knowledge'.

If we look at 1 Corinthians 12:8–10 we will find a list

of some of the spiritual gifts that God graciously gives to his people. This is not a complete list, and the gifts that are mentioned there (nine in all) are given to individual believers as the Holy Spirit decides.

> *To one there is given through the Spirit the message of wisdom, to another the message of knowledge by means of the same Spirit, to another faith by the same Spirit, to another gifts of healing by that one Spirit, to another miraculous powers, to another prophecy, to another distinguishing between spirits, to another speaking in different kinds of tongues, and to still another the interpretation of tongues (NIV).*

Notice the second in the list of gifts: 'the message of knowledge'. What did Paul (the author of 1 Corinthians) mean by the 'message' or 'word' of knowledge?

In 1985 John Wimber published his best-selling book *Power Evangelism*. This book, along with John's amazing conference on signs and wonders (in City Hall, Sheffield), completely changed my life. Indeed, I owe more to John Wimber than to any other Christian who has influenced me. The Wimber legacy in my life, and indeed in hundreds of thousands of others, has been an extremely positive and fruitful one.

Having said that, John had one habit that I found grated on my own theological understanding. This was his constant reference to the 'word of knowledge'.

To get the full flavour of John's use of this phrase we need to recall the famous story of the time when John was on an airliner. His eyes were drawn to a businessman. In the moment that he looked at him something unexpected occurred. John saw the word 'adultery' written across his face in clear letters.

As John continued to stare, the man became aware of

the unwanted intrusion. He asked John what he wanted, whereupon John received more revelation: the name 'Jane'. John leaned nervously across and asked the man, 'Does the name 'Jane' mean anything to you?'

What happened next became one of the great testimonies of the renewal that broke upon the UK churches in the 1980s. To cut a long story short, the man repented and gave his life to Christ. He told his wife there and then. She also gave her life to Christ. The couple left the plane as followers of Christ.

Many since John Wimber's time have referred to this kind of personal prophetic insight as 'the word of knowledge'. But the truth is that in New Testament times this kind of revelation was always known as prophecy. When Jesus has a very similar insight into the woman of Samaria's life she does not reply by saying, 'I see you operate in the word of knowledge.' She declares, 'I see you are a prophet.' This is because she instantly recognised what she heard as prophetic revelation. When Paul talked about the impact of prophecy on unbelievers, he wrote in 1 Corinthians 14:24–25 that the secrets of their hearts are exposed. This is exactly what happened to the businessman on the plane with John Wimber. Paul would have called that prophecy!

I believe it is really important for us to distinguish between prophecy and the words of knowledge and wisdom, as I have already argued in my two books *Know Your Spiritual Gifts* and *A Teacher's Notebook*. So what is the difference? Those who have done a lot of preaching know that there are times when words just flow out of your mouth, and oftentimes the words that come are not words you prepared or have learned from others. Wise ways of summing up complex issues suddenly come to mind. Extraordinary insights into God's nature and ways enter your consciousness seemingly from nowhere. When this happens, no one is more surprised and delighted than you are! The fact is, God is giving the gifts of wisdom and knowledge to you when this kind of thing occurs. These insights are not supposed to be kept private but are to be declared to others. That is why they are called the 'word' of wisdom and the 'word' of knowledge. They are supposed to be spoken!

So we need to remove a barrier of misunderstanding if we are to engage in prophetic evangelism. Prophecy should not be confused with the word of knowledge and the word of knowledge should not be confused with prophecy. This is now being recognised by others. Most notably, Wayne Grudem's 2000 reprint of his influential book *The Gift of Prophecy in the New Testament and Today* has followed this line of thinking (this was not in evidence in the 1988 and 1997 editions).

Miracles on the Margins

But I haven't yet shared everything that I received from the Lord in that vestry in the east end of Oslo. I sensed the Father saying something else as well.

As I reflected on the episode involving the Samaritan woman in John 4, it suddenly occurred to me how important it was that Jesus was ministering on the margins. The truth is, Jesus was not in the centre of the town: he was on the circumference. Furthermore, he was not ministering to the mainstream but to the marginalized. The woman he met on the edge of town was a woman who had almost certainly been marginalized by her own shame. She was a social outcast, looking for love in all the wrong places. Maybe she had wrecked a few marriages and broken a few hearts. She had certainly gone through five marriages herself, and not all of these could have been terminated through bereavement.

And so I sensed the Father saying something more about the use of prophecy in evangelism. I sensed him saying that he would begin this work on the margins of UK society, among those who live on the edge socially. I sensed that this work would begin among the poor, among those who are not part of the mainstream. The full revelation I received can be summed up like this:

> There will be a move of my Spirit in the coming years. It will involve the use of prophecy in evangelism. It will start on the margins with the marginalized before moving into the mainstream. If you bless what I am doing on the circumference of society, among the poor, then I will bring it into the centre too.

The real test of a prophetic word is whether it bears fruit. What has encouraged me is that since that time prophetic evangelism has indeed been emerging on the margins of society, particularly in the prisons. In fact, we have on staff at St Andrew's a clergyman called Greg Downes who spent several years as senior chaplain of a prison in Bristol (1999–2001). This is his testimony:

> Ashfield is a new prison that opened its doors on 1 November 1999. Built at a cost of £50 million, it occupies the site of what was formerly Pucklechurch Remand Centre, which was burned down by the overenthusiastic inmates in 1990. The establishment houses four hundred young persons, three hundred of whom are juveniles (15- to 17-year-olds) and one hundred young offenders (18- to 21-year-olds).

When we opened back in 1999, it was a steep learning curve for me. I recall those early days of getting 'butterflies' in my stomach on a Saturday night in anticipation of leading Sunday morning church in Ashfield.

In the first week, a boy told me that he had frightened some elderly people during an attempted house burglary.

'I really feel shame: how can I get rid of it?' he asked me.

'I know a very good way,' I replied and proceeded to tell him about Jesus.

'OK,' he said, 'I want to become a Christian.'

I explained clearly the cost of commitment and that to become a Christian was 'not a magic prayer, not the end but the beginning'.

As many young people came to faith in Christ, the attitude of the prison authorities went from indifference to being positively favourable.

There was an incident one night when I was about to leave and the assistant director came to my office and asked me to visit a young man who was suicidal. He was very depressed and had not been eating or mixing with his peers. I spoke to him in his cell and found he was so down that he was speaking in monosyllables. He shared with me that he'd made repeated attempts on his life and that since the age of fourteen he had been troubled with 'voices' telling him to kill himself. After some investigation, it turned out that he had dabbled with ouija boards and, surprise surprise, he had first done this at the age of fourteen.

After I had shared the Gospel with him, this young man gave his life to Jesus. Instantly his depression left him and he was laughing and speaking fluently. In fact, a nurse from the prison visited him straight after me and commented, 'In my opinion, this young person is no longer at risk.' The following day, he was playing football with his mates and the same assistant director said to me, 'I don't understand what you say to them, but keep it up because it works.'

Perhaps the major factor of the move of God here is that we have sometimes stepped into power evangelism, where the prophetic, words of revelation and even healing have precipitated someone giving their life to Jesus Christ.

I recall one instance when I visited a young person in the segregation block who was there for his own protection as he had been bullied by two boys on the wing. I asked him, 'Who's at home for you?' He replied that there was no one as his parents had left him and his grandfather had brought him up, but was now dead.

At this point, I sensed the Lord drop a word into my spirit and spoke it out.

'Yes, your grandfather died when you were thirteen, didn't he?'

Amazed, the boy asked how I knew this fact, as his grandfather had died on his thirteenth birthday. This was significant for him since that was when he went off the rails. His grandfather was the only person who was there for him and had shown him love.

After I told him about Jesus, this young man gave his life to Christ and experienced physical heat in his chest. He said to me, 'God spoke to me!' When I enquired further, he told me that God had told him to forgive the two boys who had beaten him up. As I was leaving, I said, 'Just out of interest, why did you become a Christian?' He replied, 'Well, if God spoke to you like that, that proves what you have said is true.'

So far, over four hundred young men have committed their lives to Christ. Clearly God is at work in our prisons. The statement of Jesus – *'the harvest is plentiful but the workers are few'* – could not be truer than in this area of much-neglected evangelical concern.

I often say that regarding the parable of the prodigal son; the young men in Ashfield know half the story. They know what it's like to be in the far country. They know what it's like to experience the bankruptcy of life. Now all they need to know is that there is a God in heaven who loves them with an everlasting love and who longs to enfold them in his divine embrace.

From Consumerism to Evangelism

I have felt for a while now that there is going to be a major spiritual harvest in the UK. This time God's power will not just be released for the refreshing of those who already know Jesus. It will be released into local communities and cities, sweeping Christians into the market place with the Gospel, and non-Christians into the worship place with a hunger for Jesus. As this harvest begins to happen, I sense that God will grant more and more of his power to his church, enabling believers to witness to the lost in miraculous ways. Time will tell, but I sense this will involve the Father giving his children a greater degree of spiritual authority and power, particularly in ministries like prophecy. These gifts have already been in evidence in churches for many years. But the truth is we have largely used them to bless one another. We have not yet used them in our outreach. What excites me is the possibility that God will pour out his Spirit upon us so that we are enabled to prophesy over those far away from God, and in the process see a great acceleration in people moving from unbelief to faith in Christ. If this happens, prophetic evangelism will play a major part in this spiritual harvest.

But there is a problem. If we go back to the story of Jesus and the Samaritan woman, the one group we omitted to mention was Jesus' disciples. They play a part in the incident in Samaria. While Jesus is witnessing prophetically to the woman, the disciples are off finding food in the town. When they come back they begin to feel guilty because they have eaten and Jesus hasn't:

> *Meanwhile, the disciples were urging Jesus to eat. 'No,' he said, 'I have food you don't know about.' 'Who brought it to him?' the disciples asked each other. Then Jesus explained: 'My nourishment comes from doing the will of God, who sent me, and from finishing his work . . .' (Jn. 4:31–34).*

What we have here is a great contrast between Jesus and his disciples. Jesus has found food of a different kind. His nourishment comes from obeying God's will for his life, to seek and save the lost. This is what Jesus is doing here. He is focusing on bringing the message of salvation to the lost. The disciples, on the other hand, are only concerned about themselves. They have been to town to find lunch. It is interesting to note that they fail to bring anyone out of the town to meet Jesus. The woman of Samaria does that!

To put it succinctly, while the disciples are into consumerism, Jesus is into evangelism. Jesus' mission statement is 'Feed them.' The disciples' is 'Feed me.'

And that's how so much of the church is today, focused on 'me and my needs'. For the church to participate in a great spiritual harvest there must be a fundamental paradigm shift from receiving a blessing to giving a blessing. Jesus said, 'Freely you have received, freely give.' John Wimber always used to say, 'You have got to give it away.' It is time for the church to start taking the blessing out of the church and sharing it with seekers and unbelievers.

Prophecy is one of the blessings the church has received. It's now time to give that away to those who don't know Jesus.

A man once testified in one of D.L. Moody's meetings that he had lived 'on the Mount of Transfiguration' for five years. 'How many souls did you lead to Christ last year?' Moody bluntly asked him.

'Well,' the man hesitated, 'I don't know.'

'Have you saved any?' Moody persisted.

'I don't know that I have,' the man admitted.

'Well,' said Moody, 'we don't want that kind of mountaintop experience. When a man gets up so high that he cannot reach down and save poor sinners, there is something wrong.'

From the Margins to the Mainstream

I firmly believe the Father is calling the church to focus on seeking and saving the lost. To obey the call we need to start taking gifts like prophecy and using them to sow into the lives of the lost. This is what Jesus did. This is what the church is being called to do. As Jesus said, in his first sermon, quoting from Isaiah 61:

The Spirit of the Lord is upon me, for he has appointed me to preach Good News to the poor. He has sent me to proclaim that captives will be released, that the blind will see, that the downtrodden will be freed from their oppressors, and that the time of the Lord's favour has come (Lk. 4:18–19).

Notice how Jesus speaks here about preaching Good News to 'the poor'. My conviction for years has been that the coming harvest would begin on the margins of society, among the poor, and that prophecy would be a vital resource in this. Prophecy can bring release, healing, liberation and favour to the poor.

I remember how a couple of years ago a friend of mine – now a Church of England vicar – found himself in a pub with a friend in north London. He had sat down to chat with his friend when a group of young men came into the pub and sat at a table nearby. After half an hour, one of the young men came over to my friend (Jonathan) and said the following words:

'I see you are a man of integrity. Do you have anything to say to me?'

Jonathan had already spotted the young man – gaunt, pale and thin – and had sensed God highlighting him. So he looked at the man and said, 'Yes. God has shown me that you are dying of Aids and that he wants you to know that he loves you.'

'That's amazing,' said the young man. 'I am dying of Aids, and I've been walking the streets of London today crying out to God, "If you're real and you're out there, please give me a sign that you care about me before this day is out."'

In that pub, Jonathan and his friend were able to talk to that young man about Jesus and pray with him.

I believe passionately that it is time to make the transition from consumerism to evangelism. In many ways the harvest has already begun on the margins, among the marginalized. A move of God is already occurring among the poor. It is now beginning to spread into the mainstream of society. One of the greatest resources in evangelism is proving to be prophetic revelation. Indeed, I sense in my spirit that the gift of prophecy will turn out to be a golden sickle in the hands of the harvesters. This should encourage us to recognise that it's time to get stuck into prophetic evangelism!

Chapter 4

PROPHECY AND PERSONAL EVANGELISM

I was recently talking to a man who has been in the prophetic ministry for many years. I asked him whether he used prophecy in evangelising unbelievers. He replied with these words: 'Oh yes, definitely. In fact, I really didn't think I could evangelise at all until I started using the gift of prophecy with unbelievers. Then I suddenly realised I could do it. Or better still, that God could do it, through me.'

Fascinated by this, I asked him how often he used the gift of prophecy in witnessing. 'Almost as often as I ask for it,' he replied. I then asked him for an example. There were many, but the one that stood out was the time he asked to sit in the cockpit of a plane on its approach to land. He had never experienced the thrill of this before and had always wanted to. These were the days before 11 September 2001, so requests like this were treated favourably. Having asked the flight attendant, my friend waited to hear the response from the cockpit.

As my friend waited, he sensed the Holy Spirit saying, 'Ask the Father for a prophecy.' This he duly did, and the following came immediately to mind: 'The pilot has two sons. One of them is a chip off the old block. He is very similar to his father. This has led to friction and it is causing the father great concern.'

When the flight attendant returned she said that the go-ahead had been given and my friend went to the front of the plane. There was some small talk and then an opportunity came to share the word. The pilot did indeed have two sons and one of them was very similar to him, causing tension. The man was overwhelmed and became very open to further words. As my friend left the cockpit after landing, the pilot grabbed hold of his hand and with tears in his eyes thanked him profusely.

Clearly, the gift of prophecy can be used with great effect in the process of evangelism. As we are obedient and sow a word into someone's life, we help that person towards the point where they can decide to follow Jesus Christ for the rest of their lives. We may not reap what we sow, but we can still sow faithfully into others' lives.

Prophecy Outside the Church

There are really two main contexts in which one can use prophecy while witnessing to those who don't know Jesus: private witnessing and public worship. In the next chapter I will look at how the gift of prophecy can be used to great effect when there are unbelievers present in public Christian worship. In this chapter I want to show how the gift can be used in private witnessing outside the church – in the workplace, the neighbourhood, the place of leisure, the home, anywhere!

Our greatest example in all of this is Jesus. Jesus used the gift of prophecy frequently as he ministered to those who were not his followers. For example, in John 1:45–51 we find Jesus prophesying over Nathanael. The context is neither the synagogue nor the Temple. In other words, Jesus is not ministering in the worship place but in the market place. We don't know exactly where Jesus is situated but it is somewhere out on the open road.

Philip went off to look for Nathanael and told him, 'We have found the very person Moses and the prophets wrote about! His name is Jesus, the son of Joseph from Nazareth.' 'Nazareth!' exclaimed Nathanael. 'Can anything good come from there?' 'Just come and see for yourself,' Philip said (Jn. 1:45–46).

What we see in this episode is a man turn from scepticism to faith in the person of Jesus Christ. This happens extremely quickly – within a matter of minutes. One minute Nathanael is proclaiming, 'Can anything good come from Nazareth?' In other words, 'How can Jesus be the Messiah if he's from that place?' The next minute he is saying to Jesus that he is the Son of God and the King of Israel. That's quite a change in perspective! And it all comes about as a direct result of Jesus' use of the gift of prophecy in evangelism. In fact, we will see after the opening of the story that Jesus has three prophetic insights about Nathanael: about his past, his present and his future.

Prophecies About the Present

As they approached, Jesus said, 'Here comes an honest man [lit: a man with 'no deceit'] – a true son of Israel.' 'How do you know about me?' Nathanael asked (Jn. 1:47-48a).

The first of the three prophetic words that Jesus has for Nathanael concerns the present. Using the present tense Jesus says, 'There is no deceit in this man.' The word 'deceit' is significant. In the Old Testament, Jacob (later named Israel) was a man who deceived others. Jesus says of Nathanael that he is a true Israelite because there is no Jacob-like deceit in him. This clearly had some special personal significance for Nathanael because he goes on to say, 'How do you know about me?'

Notice how the word Jesus gives did not reveal something negative. Jesus speaks a loving word of affirmation over Nathanael. Insights about what people are really like or what they are doing are powerful. Sometimes they are challenging and bring conviction. Sometimes they are positive and bring affirmation. Sometimes they are purely descriptive or neutral and bring a confirmation that God knows them.

In the summer of 2003 I was conducting a weekend prophetic evangelism seminar in Norway. I took a team from St Andrew's to mentor them in this method of outreach. On the first evening (Friday) we started with sung worship. I took one of the men in my team to the back of the church and asked him what he saw. Gradually the Holy Spirit started to spotlight people and reveal things about them.

One of these was a man standing near the back. I had never met or spoken to him before, but as soon as I looked at him the word 'engineer' dropped into my heart. I asked the Father to give me some more. I sensed him saying, 'He is a man who builds bridges.'

At the end of my teaching time on prophetic evangelism I asked the conference delegates to stand and I started to speak the words that we had received, believing that God would honour the faith that was being put in him!

The first man I asked to stand was the man I had had a word for. I told him what I had received, then asked him whether it made any sense. He replied that it did. He said that he was indeed an engineer and that he had sensed God calling him to build bridges in terms of reconciliation in the work place. For him it was a very powerful confirmation of what God wanted him to do.

Many other words were given that night but I draw

attention to this one because it was simply a word about what the man was doing *presently*, and it was not a word of conviction but simply a descriptive word. Very often this happens in prophesying over others. Indeed, I remember standing praying for a man I didn't know and seeing him dressed as a captain of the Royal Artillery. I then saw him firing field guns over his own soldiers into the enemy's camp and the Lord spoke to me the word 'intercession'. I told the man what I had heard and he replied, 'I used to be a captain in the Royal Artillery. I now work full time as a leader of an intercession movement!'

We need to understand that prophecies are not always predictive. They don't always point to the future. They can equally often reveal what is happening in the present. This often happens when we prophesy over fellow believers. It can be a very powerful tool when witnessing prophetically to non-Christians.

John Wright describes how the Lord gave him just one word for a non-Christian. He writes:

My father-in-law is a General who once taught a Pakistani Major I will call Mohammed at a military academy. This young man clearly benefited from my father-in-law's instruction, as he later became a Brigadier General and Ambassador for Pakistan to a number of countries.

After his retirement at the age of seventy, Mohammed came to stay with us. He proved to be a devout Muslim and got up at daybreak to say his prayers. Later we went for a walk and I invited him to tell me about Islam. He was delighted. So for the next mile or so I learnt a lot about his faith – a faith in which peace with God only comes through keeping laws.

As we neared home, I began to panic – he was not going to ask me to talk about my Christian faith. But then he paused for breath; at last I was able to get a word in edgeways. It was a question undoubtedly inspired by the Holy Spirit.

'Do you call God Father?'

'No, no,' he replied sternly. 'Creator! Creator!'

'That is the difference between us,' I said, 'because Christians call God "Father". We have a relationship with him as children, and he speaks to us!'

It was all very well to say this, but how to prove it? At the end of Mark's gospel it says that the disciples went out to proclaim the Good News and the Lord worked with them and confirmed what they were saying with signs and wonders. But could God provide a sign for Mohammed with only half a mile to go?

At that moment two girls in their mid-twenties appeared, walking towards us. I stopped to introduce my distinguished visitor, at the same time asking the Holy Spirit to tell me what Juliet, the girl I was talking to, did for a living. In my mind came the thought nurse, so I launched out hopefully.

'Ah, Juliet,' I said, 'I hear you are a nurse.'

Juliet's face fell with astonishment as she looked down to see what bit of a nurse's uniform had given the game away. But there was nothing to see.

'Well, yes, actually we are both nurses,' she said. 'But how did you know?'

I gave her a reassuring smile and explained.

'Well, I am a Christian and my Father in heaven told me as a sign to General Mohammed that the Christian God is alive and speaks to his children.'

The looks on the faces of the General and the two nurses were wonderful to behold as we continued our walk home.

Prophetic insights about the present can be extremely powerful in evangelism. As in the case of my friend in the cockpit of the aeroplane, revelation about what is happening in a person's life right *now* can open them up to the reality of God very quickly.

Prophecies About the Past

> *And Jesus replied, 'I could see you under the fig tree before Philip found you.' Nathanael replied, 'Teacher, you are the Son of God – the King of Israel!' (Jn. 1:48b–49).*

As I have already said, not all prophecy points to the future. Actually, a person operating in the gift of prophecy may see something that happened in the past. Here, Jesus has a word of revelation about what Nathanael has been doing in the recent past.

What is it that Jesus saw? Jesus saw Nathanael sitting all alone under a fig tree just before Philip came running to get him. What was Nathanael doing? The commentaries go running in all directions at this point. Speculation abounds as people try to guess what Nathanael was up to. The truth is, we will never know until heaven what Nathanael was doing. We do know that sitting under a fig tree was something rabbis did when they wanted to read the Scriptures. Maybe Nathanael was reading the story of Jacob's prophetic dream. That is my personal view but I cannot prove it, and I am now demonstrating the same speculative tendencies I have just criticised in others! Whatever the case, Nathanael was amazed. No one else had been there, yet Jesus had seen him. This shows Nathanael that Jesus is more than just a man, more even than just a great teacher. He is the Son of God and the King of Israel!

Prophetic insights into the details of a seeker's past can be a powerful means of making them more receptive to the Gospel. In the last chapter I mentioned my friend Greg Downes, on the staff at St Andrew's but formerly senior chaplain of a prison. He saw hundreds come to Christ through prophetic evangelism.

> On one occasion I was escorting a young offender back to the hospital wing from Sunday morning Chapel. As we walked, out of the blue, the Lord spoke to me about this young man so I spoke it out:
>
> 'You were tempted to commit suicide last night. . . at nine o'clock.'
>
> The young man had indeed been tempted to take his own life at exactly that time due to despair and depression, having entered prison full of fear for the first time that day. He suddenly realised that Jesus is alive, knew all about him and cared deeply for him. The young man surrendered his life to Christ and the transformation in him was instant and radical.

We need to be open to prophetic words about people's past when we are witnessing to them. Prophecy isn't just future-focused.

Take another example.

A friend of mine who is now a clergyman has often been used by God to prophesy into the lives of those who don't come to church, with extraordinary results.

Recently he took his wife out to a hotel for a meal. A couple on a table nearby got engaged in conversation with them and took a liking to them. After they had all finished their meal, the couple invited my friend and his wife to come and have a coffee in the bar. My friend and his wife accepted.

As soon as they sat down, my friend received a word for the man that (to use his own phrase) absolutely 'nailed him'. The Lord showed him that the man had been married before, that this was his second marriage, and that he was still reeling from the effects of his divorce.

My friend calmly shared this revelation in the form of questions.

'You've been married before, haven't you?'

'Yes, that's amazing. How did you know?'

'And you haven't recovered from the trauma of your first marriage breaking up, have you?'

'That's even more amazing. How did you know *that*?'

'God has just told me, and he has also told me to tell you to come back to him.'

'That's incredible. I'm a lapsed Christian. I used to go to church a lot.'

Needless to say, these prophetic insights into the man's past life opened the door to sharing the wonderful Good News of Jesus.

I say again, we must be open to receiving revelation about the secret past history of unbelievers we meet, not just their future history.

Prophecies About the Future

Jesus asked him, 'Do you believe all this just because I told you I had seen you under the fig tree? You will see greater things than this.' Then he said, 'The truth is, you will all see heaven open and the angels of God going up and down upon the Son of Man' (Jn. 1:50–51).

In these verses Jesus prophesies about Nathanael's future. This is an important characteristic of prophecy.

While it is simplistic to equate prophecy with the future, prophecy sometimes does disclose what is to come in a person's life. When this happens, prophecy releases hope by showing that God indeed knows the plans that he has for our lives. In fact, this is one of the most powerful consequences of the prophetic. Genuine prophecy brings hope to those who need it. It highlights that every day of our lives is recorded in God's book (Ps. 139:16) and that the Lord will work out his plans for our lives (Ps. 138:8).

What Jesus tells Nathanael is that he is going to see 'even greater things' than those he has already seen. What has Nathanael already seen? This is disclosed in verse 49, where Nathanael says, 'Teacher, you are the Son of God – the King of Israel!' Here we see Nathanael acknowledging who Jesus really is. This should always be the end result of true prophecy – the revelation of the glory of Jesus Christ.

It is this revelation that Jesus promises will be superseded in the future. Jesus says (this is my own paraphrase):

> *'Nathanael, you have already seen some great things. But you haven't seen anything compared with what is to come. You are going to come under an open heaven. There you will see the true majesty of the Son of Man, the mediator between heaven and earth. As with Jacob's ladder, the Son of Man will have angels ascending and descending upon him.'*

What is interesting here is that Jesus, having used prophecy in witnessing to Nathanael, now promises Nathanael that he will himself be a prophet. Nathanael will see more clearly who Jesus is. Personally, I believe that Jesus is referring not just to one vision but to many. I also believe that he is referring not to the life to come but to this life. In effect he is saying to Nathanael, you are going to have the gift of prophecy. Nathanael is going to see pictures and visions of the matchless supremacy of Jesus Christ.

So Jesus uses prophecy in witnessing to Nathanael, and this prophecy unveils something of Nathanael's destiny in God.

Jesus used future-oriented prophecy in his witness to others in the Gospels:

> *Looking intently at Simon, Jesus said, 'You are Simon, the son of John – but you will be called Cephas' (which means Peter) (Jn. 1:42).*

> *Jesus replied to Simon, 'Don't be afraid! From now on you'll be fishing for people!' (Lk. 5:10).*

There is no doubt that prophetic words can release a sense of destiny and direction to people's lives. I recall a time when I was ministering in Sweden and the pastor of a church asked me to pray for a group of young adults. The first person I looked at was a man in his late twenties. As I looked at him I saw him dressed as a clown. I then asked the Father for more and he started to give me words about the man being an effective communicator, who got people's attention through humour. I then received a further word about him being raised up to preach the Gospel, that unchurched people would be touched by his words, and that he would use humour in a wise way to soften the hearts of his listeners.

As I gave this word, all the other church members started laughing. I asked the pastor what was the matter. He said that the man indeed had a great sense of humour and was something of a comedian. He also said that in recent months he had recognised that the man had a calling to preach and, in the last few weeks, had given him the opportunity to do so before the whole church. Evidently he had been very well received, not least because of his sense of humour.

Prophesying over fellow believers can therefore have a future focus. The same can also be true when we use prophecy with unbelievers, though we should note one thing: future-oriented prophecy is not as potent as prophecies about people's past and present. The simple reason for this is because future prophecy is not immediately verifiable. You have to wait for its fulfilment.

Having said that, I recall when a member of my church was walking down a road in Chorleywood and met some non-Christian neighbours outside their house. My friend sensed anxiety, so stopped and talked with them. It turned out they could not sell their house. Straight away the Holy Spirit dropped a word into my friend's heart: 'I sense God is saying that you will have sold your house within two weeks.' Exactly fourteen days later, against all the odds, the house was sold. The couple told my friend they were now sorry they were moving. They would have liked to start coming to services at St Andrew's!

Future-oriented prophecy can therefore be used in evangelism. Obviously we need to take enormous care here. Most of us could tell horror stories of times when prophecy has been misused. Directional words about people getting married or having children have sometimes been uttered out of wish-fulfilment rather than a genuine word from God. The damage this causes is quite awful and often permanent. There is therefore a great need to exercise honesty and discernment when giving words about a person's future. We must ensure that the word is motivated by the Holy Spirit and not by our quite natural desire to see people blessed. Extra care should always be taken over future-focused words, whether for believers or unbelievers.

Using the Salt Cellar

Jesus receives prophetic insights into Nathanael's character (you are a man without deceit), his conduct (I saw you under the fig tree) and his calling (you will see even greater things). As Jesus utters these prophetic insights, Nathanael turns from a sceptic to a believer. Within a few minutes, he goes from asking, 'Can anything good come from Nazareth?' (v. 46) to, 'Teacher, you are the Son of God, the King of Israel' (v. 49).

The purpose of prophecy in evangelism is to evoke faith in Jesus. To put it another way, prophetic words function like salt. They make unbelievers thirsty for Jesus. Paul says in Colossians 4:5–6:

> *Be wise in the way you act towards outsiders; make the most of every opportunity. Let your conversation be always full of grace, seasoned with salt, so that you may know how to answer everyone (NIV).*

When we use prophetic words in evangelism, we are effectively sowing salt into people's hearts, making them thirsty for the living water that only Jesus offers.

Mention of living water brings me back to the story we looked at in the previous chapter, Jesus' witness to the Samaritan woman at the well (Jn. 4:4–42). It is very interesting to look in that chapter to the developing revelation of Jesus in the woman's life:

> *'You are a Jew, and I am a Samaritan woman' (Jn. 4:9).*

> *'Sir,' the woman said, 'you must be a prophet' (Jn. 4:19).*

> *'Come and meet a man who told me everything I ever did! Can this be the Messiah?' (Jn. 4:29).*

What is it that causes the quantum leap from 'You are a Jew' to 'Sir, I see you are a prophet', and then to 'Could this be the Messiah?' Quite simply, it is Jesus' use of prophecy (vv. 17–18). The woman saw this as a miracle.

The Miracle of Prophecy

There are many ways in which God speaks to both believers and unbelievers alike. The way these prophecies come to people will vary. In the story of Jesus' ministry to Nathanael we can only guess at how these revelations came to him. When Jesus saw that Nathanael was a man in whom there was no deceit, maybe this 'seeing' came in the form of a sudden impression. When Jesus saw Nathanael under the fig tree, maybe this 'seeing' came in the form of a vision or a picture, possibly even a dream. When Jesus told Nathanael about his future, maybe this 'seeing' came in the form of a Scripture passage (Jacob's dream in Genesis 28) or a message. Again, we can only really speculate.

Whatever way revelation comes to us, if it is genuine it is always miraculous. When a believer sees clearly into the secrets of an unbeliever's heart, this is certainly miraculous. When an unbeliever has a revelation that leads them to Jesus, this also is miraculous. Sudden insights like these, inspired by the Holy Spirit, come under the category of miracles. For that reason we shouldn't really call the turning of water into wine in John 2 the first miracle in John's gospel. The first miracle is really what Jesus reveals about Nathanael. The first great wonder of this gospel is Jesus' prophetic insights into the secrets of Nathanael's heart.

I believe we need to be open to God using us in miraculous ways when we are outside the four walls of the church, relating to unbelievers and seekers. Obviously we will not necessarily receive prophecies for unbelievers on a daily basis. Nor will we receive prophetic words 'on tap', as it were. If prophetic revelation is miraculous, then by definition we will probably receive it suddenly and intermittently. A miracle is, after all, an exceptional not an everyday event. If it occurred every day, then it would cease to evoke awe and wonder! Nevertheless, miracles do happen. The Father does speak to us about those who don't yet know him. The Father also speaks directly into the lives of those who are far from him but whom he is calling into a saving relationship with himself.

The big factor in determining whether or not we are used in prophetic evangelism will be our mindset. If we have a mindset that says that prophecy is not for today, or not for me, then we will almost certainly miss out on this wonderful method of evangelism. If we operate with the mindset that says that prophecy is only for believers in the church, we will almost certainly miss out on using this gift in evangelism. The Bible says that as a person thinks in their heart, so they are (Prov. 23:7, KJV). If we think in the wrong way, we will act in the wrong way. Our beliefs directly affect our behaviour.

I would like to encourage every believer reading this book to think biblically about prophetic evangelism. Believe that the gift of prophecy is for today. Believe that you can not only desire the gift of prophecy but also receive it. Believe that you too can receive revelation about the secrets of seekers' hearts. As the song goes, 'there can be miracles when you believe'. Use the Scriptures and testimonies in this book to build your faith in God's ability to speak through you prophetically. Faith is like a muscle. It grows stronger through exercise. Exercise your faith in God's ability to give you prophecies in personal evangelism. He is faithful!

Chapter 5

USING PROPHECY IN SEEKER SERVICES

In the previous chapter we looked at using prophecy in personal evangelism. But one-to-one witnessing is not the only context for prophetic evangelism. The New Testament shows that there are two main contexts: first, *private witnessing*, second, *public worship*. In this chapter I want to look at how we can use prophetic words to evangelise seekers during public worship.

The key passage for all of this is in 1 Corinthians 14. This chapter as a whole deals with the gifts of the Spirit, and gives special emphasis to the gift of tongues and the gift of prophecy.

Paul begins by stating, 'Let love be your highest goal, but also desire the special abilities the Spirit gives, especially the gift of prophecy' (v. 1). We should note the fact that we are to desire the gifts of the Spirit and we are particularly to set our hearts on pursuing the gift of prophecy. Why does Paul emphasize prophecy? It seems that the church members in Corinth were using tongues without interpretation in public worship. The reason for this was that they regarded the gift of tongues as the highest of all the gifts. Those who were giving Paul a hard time were saying 'pursue especially the gift of tongues'. This had led to an unbridled and insensitive use of the gift in public worship.

Paul counters this not by saying that the gift of tongues is worthless but by arguing that the gift of prophecy is superior because it is intelligible. Tongues without interpretation are of limited value. Having said that, with interpretation, the gift of tongues can be of immense value. When someone speaks in an unlearned foreign language, as a direct result of the work of the Holy Spirit, it can lead to life-changing results.

Consider the following example reported in the summer of 2003 by *Joy* magazine.

Mattersey Hall Bible College Principal David Petts had a remarkable double surprise shortly after he spoke a few words in tongues while illustrating his teaching from the pulpit recently.

'I was preaching in Newark Assemblies of God Church on the Baptism in the Spirit,' says David. 'As I often do when speaking on this subject, I said that speaking in tongues is something you yourself do – and spoke a few words in tongues to illustrate this. Then I carried on teaching in English.

'After the meeting a woman came up to me and said, "I'm embarrassed to tell you I understood the language you spoke when you spoke in tongues." I was thrilled that she'd recognised the language but wondered why she was embarrassed!

'She went on to tell me she was a gypsy and spoke the gypsy language of Romany. She said that only that morning her husband had told her that she should give up smoking. Like many travelling people, she had a problem in that area and felt she needed some divine help to give up.

'She then said, "Imagine my amazement that when you spoke in tongues you actually spoke in Romany and said 'I have told you cigarettes are not good!'"

'I prayed for her and haven't seen her since, but the pastor of Newark vouches for the fact she is a good reliable woman who isn't likely to make things up. So I saw a double miracle – first that I spoke Romany (which I've no knowledge of) and also that God used tongues to speak to someone (as in Acts 2).'

The gift of tongues, when it is interpreted (as in the story above), can be of immense value. But this was clearly not what was going on in Corinth. In the Corinthian church, people were speaking in tongues without interpretation and it seems they were doing it to show off how spiritual they were. Paul writes in response to this by arguing that they should make prophecy their priority, not tongues. Paul argues that prophecy is superior to uninterpreted tongues because with tongues you are using unintelligible speech, whereas with prophecy you're using language that can be understood. Indeed, prophecy can benefit everyone because it builds up, encourages and comforts the church. The gift of tongues merely edifies the person speaking, whereas the gift of prophecy edifies everyone.

The Mature Use of the Gifts

At this point (1 Cor. 14:20) Paul calls for maturity in the church's understanding and handling of the gifts of the Spirit. He says that it is perfectly permissible to be childlike in certain matters. He highlights evil as the place where a holy naivety is called for. But in connection with gifts like tongues and prophecy he calls for maturity. He says that believers are to behave like full-grown adults and steward these gifts with sense and sensitivity.

Paul now starts to speak in a very complex way about the gift of tongues. Using a passage from the Old Testament (Is. 28:11–12), Paul justifies his call to maturity by saying that those who speak in tongues during worship need to take great care. If unbelievers are present, uninterpreted tongues can have a devastating consequence. Unbelievers will look at such behaviour and say, 'I came in here thinking that Christians were a strange sect; now I think they are a bunch of raving lunatics.' In thinking such thoughts, unbelievers will effectively find themselves farther from God than they were before they came to the meeting.

It is for this reason that Paul makes the strange comment that uninterpreted tongues function as a sign for unbelievers (v. 22). Now we automatically associate the word 'sign' with miracles. So we make the mistake of thinking that 'sign' here is a positive word. But this is not how Paul is thinking at all. He is using the word 'sign' here in a negative sense. Sign in this context does not mean a *plus* sign but a *minus* sign. It means a sign of God's judgement and displeasure. Unbelievers, judging Christians to be maniacs on the basis of their exposure to tongues, themselves come under judgement. As such, tongues are a sign, yes, but not a sign of something good but something very, very bad.

Here again Paul is trying to get the Corinthians to see that in public worship prophecy is a gift that is superior to tongues without interpretation. He offers two main reasons in the argument of verses 22–25. To see what these are, we need to quote the passage in full:

So you see that speaking in tongues is a sign, not for believers, but for unbelievers; prophecy, however, is for the benefit of believers, not unbelievers. Even so, if unbelievers or people who don't understand these things come into your meeting and hear everyone talking in an unknown language, they will think you are crazy. But if all of you are prophesying, and

> *unbelievers or people who don't understand these things come into your meeting, they will be convicted of sin, and they will be condemned by what you say. As they listen, their secret thoughts will be laid bare, and they will fall down on their knees and worship God, declaring, 'God is really here among you' (1 Cor. 14:22–25).*

The first reason why prophecy is superior to tongues is because prophecy is a positive sign. Uninterpreted tongues function as a negative or minus sign in the lives of unbelievers because they result in unbelievers deriding the church and coming under even greater judgement. Prophecy, on the other hand, is a positive or a plus sign but it functions in this way primarily for believers rather than unbelievers. As I stated in the introduction, the absence of prophecy among God's people was seen in the Old Testament as a sign of God's disfavour. The presence of prophecy was seen as a sign of God's pleasure. If God's people are operating in the gift of prophecy during worship, it means that God's favour and pleasure are upon them. This, for God's people, makes the gift of prophecy a very positive sign. It means God is present, and nothing is more important for believers than that. For believers, then, prophecy is a *plus*!

The second reason why prophecy is superior to uninterpreted tongues is because of its effect on unbelievers. Prophecy is a sign for believers, yes, but even so it affects unbelievers positively as well. Whereas uninterpreted tongues result in unbelievers being more hostile to God, prophecy results in them being more receptive to God. Prophecy causes unbelievers to declare 'Truly God is among you.' In other words, it results in lost people acknowledging God's reality and presence.

All in all, Paul argues that spiritual maturity in

relation to the gifts is a matter of a right assessment of the merits of prophecy above uninterpreted tongues in public worship. He offers a number of reasons why the Corinthians should be more positive about the use of prophecy than about the use of uninterpreted tongues. We should remind ourselves that Paul is talking about the use of these gifts in public worship.

Prophecy	Tongues (Uninterpreted)
To the church	To God only
Others benefit	Only the speaker benefits
Intelligible	Mysterious
Strengthens the church	Strengthens the person
Usually clear	Unclear
Engages mind and spirit	Engages spirit only
Positive effect on the lost	Negative effect on the lost

A mature Christian, Paul argues, understands these things and adjusts their public behaviour accordingly.

The Power of Prophecy

From the discussion above it should be very clear that prophetic words have a really important place in public worship. Prophecies, when they are accurate, are first of all fruitful in the lives of believers. As Paul says in 1 Corinthians 14:3, 'One who prophesies is helping others grow in the Lord, encouraging and comforting them.'

Prophecy secondly has a very fruitful effect in the lives of unbelievers. Paul does not see public worship as a Christians-only event. He knew that unbelievers came into such meetings. He allows believers to prophesy when unbelievers are present because of prophecy's life-changing consequences. If prophecy results in comfort for believers, it results in conviction for unbelievers.

Why does prophecy have such a powerful effect on unbelievers in church? To answer that question we need to go right back to the very beginning of the Bible and indeed to the beginning of history. Before the Fall, Adam and Eve were able to stand in the presence of God (and in each other's presence) naked and unashamed. But when they sinned, they were no longer able to be so free. In fact, they went into hiding. We read in Genesis 3:7–9:

> *At that moment, their eyes were opened, and they suddenly felt shame at their nakedness. So they strung fig leaves together around their hips to cover themselves. Towards evening they heard the LORD God walking about in the garden, so they hid themselves among the trees. The LORD God called to Adam, 'Where are you?'*

What has this got to do with prophecy in public worship? Simply this, that when believers receive revelation from God about unbelievers, their words are like God's word to Adam and Eve, calling them out of hiding. John writes in his gospel that unbelievers 'hate the light because they want to sin in the darkness. They stay away from the light for fear their sins will be exposed and they will be punished' (Jn. 3:20). Paul says in Ephesians 5:12–14:

> *It is shameful even to talk about the things that ungodly people do in secret. But when the light shines on them, it becomes clear how evil these things are. And where your light shines, it will expose their evil deeds.*

When prophetic words are given in a church worship service, they can have a potent effect on unbelievers. For them it is like a piercing spotlight from heaven being shone into the darkness of their lives. This in turn results in the disclosure of what they've done and the exposure of who they are.

For Paul, then, prophecy in public worship can be a really effective means of evangelising unbelieving visitors. When prophetic words hit the mark, they function like the call of God to Adam and Eve in the garden. Unbelievers experience a profound sense of conviction. Like Adam and Eve after the Fall, they feel naked and ashamed and long to get right with God. In fact, Paul is extremely specific about the potent effects of such prophetic words. He lists three internal or invisible results and three external or visible results:

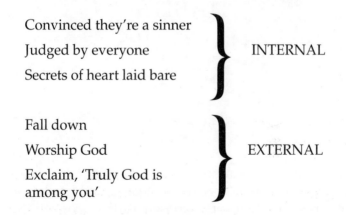

Convinced they're a sinner

Judged by everyone   } INTERNAL

Secrets of heart laid bare

Fall down

Worship God   } EXTERNAL

Exclaim, 'Truly God is
among you'

Handling Prophecy with Care

Prophecy is a very important gift in public worship. It brings comfort to believers and conviction to unbelievers. Indeed, prophecy can lead unbelievers to acknowledging their need of salvation and receiving God's free gift of pardon at the Cross. When unbelievers walk into a public worship event where the Holy Spirit is present, they come in with a concealed history of sins, wounds and addictions. This is what Paul means by the 'secrets of their hearts'. These are the things known only to God and perhaps, at best, to one or two trusted loved ones. Unbelievers enter God's presence with hearts desperately troubled by what J. John calls 'hurts, habits and hang-ups':

HURTS
HABITS
HANG-UPS

Prophetic revelation uncovers these things and leads unbelievers to seek forgiveness, healing and freedom at the Cross. Unbelievers exposed to the prophetic in worship will say to themselves, 'he's talking to me', or 'she's been reading my mail'. Prophecy has an extraordinarily powerful effect on the unredeemed heart.

In the light of this, we need to write on this gift the words 'handle with care'. When believers exercise the gift of prophecy in worship, they are uncovering the secrets of people's hearts. This means that they need to use the gift with great responsibility, wisdom and care. If Paul is strong about how to use the gift of tongues in public, he is just as strong about how to use the gift of prophecy. Just as tongues used irresponsibly can drive people away from God, so can the unwise use of prophecy. So Paul lays down some guidelines in 1 Corinthians 14:26–33.

The most salient points have to do with using prophecy in a way that promotes orderly worship. Paul knows that disorderly worship is a bad witness because God is not the author of confusion but rather of peace. So he first of all stresses the need for two or three people to prophesy at one time. This does not mean only two or three prophecies in a meeting. It means two or three people prophesying in sequence, then gifted people weighing and discerning the value of those prophecies. Then others may have a go once the first two or three have been tested. Once the second cluster of two or three words has been given, these need to be weighed too.

The next thing Paul stresses is that a person who is prophesying must stop if someone else receives a revelation while they are speaking. I believe what Paul is encouraging here is brevity. He is essentially warning against speaking for too long. A prophetic revelation can be spoken out quickly. It does not require a great sermon. If someone spends too long giving their word, the next person who receives a revelation has every right to stand and signal to the leader that they have a word. The leader can then encourage the person speaking to complete what they have been sharing. If the leader is not happy about the prophecy (because of its length) he may want to say something like this to the congregation: 'Let's just hold that last prophecy . . .'
The final thing that Paul stresses is that every person receiving prophecy is fully in control of when they deliver it and how! Perhaps the most important thing Paul says here is

in verse 32: 'Remember that people who prophesy are in control of their spirit and can wait their turn.' Paul is speaking here about the person who receives a word and who then interrupts the meeting because they supposedly can't help it. He may also be referring to people who receive a word and then deliver it in an ecstatic, 'out-of-control' manner. I have led meetings in the past where I have seen both. When a person interrupts a meeting, or delivers a prophecy in a wild manner, I give a gentle but firm reminder that people who prophesy are in control of their spirits.

This last point is really crucial when we are thinking about the impact of prophecy on unbelievers. When we are in a place of public worship, and God is moving by his Spirit, those who are particularly prone to responding in an extravagant way need to be wise. I often quote the great healing evangelist Smith Wigglesworth here. When asked whether he was always affected by the power of the Spirit, he replied: 'I am drunk in the Holy Spirit all of the time, except in the presence of unbelievers, when I restrain myself for their sakes.' That's the right balance! Filled to overflowing with the power of God at all times, yet careful not to exhibit any insensitive behaviour when non-Christians are nearby.

When people give a prophecy there are therefore guidelines for handling the gift sensitively. Below are a few obvious guidelines. In Appendix 1 you will find a fuller list. But we need to remember in the prophetic to *handle with care*.

- **Speak Audibly:** Make sure others can hear what you say.
- **Speak Calmly:** Don't get out of control. Avoid hype and hysteria.
- **Speak Normally:** Don't be *weird*. Don't be theatrical, use distracting gestures, or use old-fashioned language.

- **Speak Briefly:** Just say what is relevant. If you ramble, people will lose interest or feel angry. Just *keep to the point*.
- **Speak Humbly:** Don't be proud. You cannot exercise authority unless you are under authority. Always be willing to have your words tested: your words are not beyond error.
- **Speak Honestly:** Don't make it up or borrow someone else's word, and don't imitate someone else either!
- **Speak Lovingly:** The golden rule: speak in a tender way. Compassion, not condemnation, should be the primary quality. Be sensitive.

Using Prophecy in Seeker Services

One of the most pressing questions today has to do with how we handle prophecy in services that are designed for the unchurched. These worship events are often called 'seeker services'. They are usually low-risk meetings for those who don't know Christ. Often the worship songs will be carefully selected so they have a chance of being known to newcomers. The preaching will be geared to the actual needs of seekers and will therefore have a high relevance factor. There will sometimes be testimony. Usually there will be a good deal of multimedia and multisensory input, with drama, video, performance songs, mime and other creative media. All of this will be carefully designed to create what Bill Hybels calls 'a safe place for a dangerous message'.

How should we handle the gift of prophecy in such services? There are, as I see it, five basic options on a spectrum.

There is first of all what I call the **Prophecy-free Zone**.

Some people believe that the gift of prophecy died out at the end of the first century, after the death of the apostles. This view is known as 'Cessationism'. For this reason they will not permit words of revelation from the Body of Christ during any services, let alone seeker or guest services. I know people who honestly hold this view. I have explained why I do not believe it to be correct in my book *Know Your Spiritual Gifts.*

While some leaders disallow prophecy on Cessationist grounds, others disallow it on grounds of seeker sensitivity. When it comes to seeker services they say that we have to sacrifice things like prophecy for the sake of unbelievers. Some churches that used to be charismatic, having gone down the seeker-sensitive road, have ceased to operate publicly in gifts like prophecy and healing. In my opinion, churches that opt for this approach cease to be 'charismatic' in any root sense of the word. Charismatic comes from the Greek word *charismata*, meaning grace gifts (e.g. healing, miracles, prophecy, tongues etc). If these gifts are not publicly exercised, the church is not charismatic.

Personally I understand very well why leaders find public prophecy too great a risk during seeker services, but there are ways to minimise the dangers and to maximise the possibility of what Paul was talking about in 1 Corinthians 14:24–25. In other words, we can steward this gift in such a way that unbelievers can be powerfully impacted by it rather than turned away.

The second option is what I call **During the Sermon Only.** This means allowing prophecy but having it delivered only during the sermon.

Now once again there can be different reasons why this happens. A leader may take the view that prophecy died out in the first century and that preaching has now taken its place. In other words, prophets in New Testament times declared the word of the Lord. Now that we have the Bible we have the Word of God. The preacher who faithfully expounds and declares the Word of God does today what the prophet did in the first century. We therefore don't need prophets prophesying any more.

Again I have countered this view in my book *A Teacher's Notebook*. Let me just say that the decisive argument against this is the New Testament distinction between the gift of teaching (expounding God's written Word) and the gift of prophecy (receiving and declaring God's spontaneously revealed word). The New Testament does not confuse prophecy and preaching/teaching. Nor should we.

While some leaders may equate prophecy with preaching on theological grounds, others may do so on pastoral grounds. I know leaders who believe in the gift of prophecy but who say that they alone are going to exercise this gift and will do so during their preaching. This may be very low-key, delivered with words like 'there may be some of you here today who ...' or it may be much more overt and direct. The great nineteenth-century preacher Charles Spurgeon was a master of the more direct approach. On one occasion Spurgeon was at Exeter Hall when he suddenly stopped what he was preaching and pointed at someone saying, 'Young man, those gloves you're wearing were not paid for; you stole them from your boss!'

The young man came up to Spurgeon after the meeting in a state of shock and placed the gloves on a table, saying, 'It's the first time I have stolen from my employer, and the last. . . . Please don't tell him. It would kill my mother if she knew about this.'

Spurgeon is said to have done this sort of thing from time to time in his preaching ministry. The effect was invariably one of repentance, leading in most cases to the person he spoke to committing their lives to the Lord Jesus Christ.

Again, while I understand very well why a leader

may restrict the use of prophecy to the pulpit, this is not the New Testament way. Paul in 1 Corinthians 14:20–25 paints a picture of all believers being able to prophesy when unbelievers are present. He did not say anything about restricting such words to the sermon only.

The third option is the **Pastor as Filter** approach. Here the method consists of allowing prophecy in seeker services but disallowing spontaneous utterance of the same. Usually the leaders of the church stand at the front and, during the worship songs or some other suitable part of the meeting, those who have received a word come forward and present them with what they have seen and heard. The leaders then weigh these prophecies and, at a point later on in the worship service, filter those words they feel are accurate in a low-key way.

This is nearer to the model of 1 Corinthians 14:20–25 but it is still not quite what Paul described. On a positive note, members of the church are being encouraged to listen to God. On a negative note, they are only allowed to receive these words; they are not allowed to speak them. While this may sometimes prevent waffle, at other times vital elements of their prophecies may be lost in translation as the pastor relays them.

The fourth option is the **Authorised Group** approach. This involves having a special prophetic ministry team trained, led and authorised by the leadership team of a church. This group will consist of those who have grown mature in the prophetic and who have a good track record of hearing God. Such a group is able to function like a school of prophets.

With a prophetic ministry team a church leader can allow a greater quantity of spontaneous prophetic utterances in services designed for seekers. Though there is still an element of risk, at least the leader is permitting the prophets to prophesy! Furthermore, this group – with the right training – can also be entrusted to weigh their prophecies (a responsibility they can share with the leadership team). The downside is the danger of this group becoming an elitist clique within the church. This can create a sense of feeling worthless in the rest of the body, and feelings of pride in the group itself. There are ways round this, but it is still a possible disadvantage of the model.

The fifth and final option (as I see it) is what I call the **Free-for-All** approach. This means leaving space in the service when any member of the church (*not visitors*) can listen to God and share what they hear. Some charismatic churches use this approach in seeker services. In other words, they make no adjustments at all and they let anyone who is a member have a go. The plus side of this approach is that words really can hit the mark and lead seekers to acknowledge, 'Truly God is among you'. The minus side is that sometimes we have to listen to an awful lot of waffle, religious jargon and even silliness before we get there! So while the 'free-for-all approach' may look like the closest thing to what Paul describes in 1 Corinthians 14:20–25, it may also not be what Paul himself would advocate today!

So, looking at the spectrum of options, these are the five possibilities:

Low Risk				**High Risk**
1	2	3	4	5
Prophecy-free zone	During the sermon only	Pastor as filter	Authorised group	Free-for-all

What Would Paul Have Done?

This is a great question to ask – an alternative to WWJD, 'What Would Jesus Do?'

What would Paul have done about using prophecy in seeker services? The answer involves a degree of speculation but I believe Paul would have supported option 3 (the Pastor as Filter) or 4 (the Authorised Group).

Before we look at these two options, we need to answer why Paul might not have gone for option 5. Surely 1 Corinthians 14 is describing a free-for-all approach? Surely Paul is talking about every believer being free to prophesy in turn?

There is no doubt that this is true. But there is one vital difference between the services he is talking about and modern-day seeker services. If we look at the context of 1 Corinthians 14 we will see that Paul is talking about worship meetings that are for believers. He is not talking about services that are actually designed for unbelievers. Paul did not teach at all about seeker services in 1 Corinthians or anywhere else, though he himself engaged in meetings designed to win seekers, as the book of Acts demonstrates. In 1 Corinthians 14, Paul is describing worship meetings for believers that unbelievers happen to come into. Look at how Paul puts it in verse 24: 'If all of you are prophesying, and unbelievers or people who don't understand these things come into your meeting, they will be convicted . . .' These are not the words of someone who is describing meetings designed to attract unbelievers. These are the words of someone describing believers' meetings into which unbelievers just happen to come! That is why he says *'if'* unbelievers come in, not *'when'*.

This major difference has to be borne in mind as we consider how to use prophecy in guest or seeker services.

In worship meetings that are purely for believers I would always encourage every member of the church to have a go at hearing the Lord and speaking out what they receive. Sometimes unbelievers are present when this happens and their lives are changed.

At a regular Sunday morning service at St Andrew's in 2002 we came to the time in the meeting when we listen to the Father and speak out words of revelation. One of the words received from a church member was about a young man who had come in with a badly scratched eye. It just happened that a young man had come to church for the first time that morning. He was staying with a friend who occasionally brought his mother to church. That morning was such a morning, so this totally unchurched man found himself in a meeting where prophecies were being uttered. He was the man with the scratched eye.

After the service the young man came forward. He demanded to know who had told us about the scratched eye. Of course, Jesus had, so we told him that. This absolutely amazed him. He immediately became receptive to hearing the Gospel and, after a brief explanation of the Good News, he gave his life to the Lord!

I truly believe that this is what Paul is talking about in 1 Corinthians 14:20–25. Paul is talking there about worship meetings for believers into which unbelievers come. In such meetings, as the people of God prophesy, unbelievers find that the hidden things in their lives – hang-ups, hurts and habits – are exposed. This acts as what Paul calls a 'demonstration' or 'proof' of the Spirit's power (1 Corinthians 2:1–5, NIV). This in turn confirms the truth of the Good News and helps people to receive salvation.

At the same time, churches now run services that are designed for those who don't know Jesus Christ. Paul is *not* talking about such events in 1 Corinthians 14. At our church we design services that are specifically geared towards unbelievers in our locality. These might be anything from a service based around the movies (see my book *The Big Picture*, co-authored with J. John), or a Christmas carol service, which hundreds of unchurched people attend. What we have found is that the free-for-all approach is not wise in such meetings. Those who are not mature in the gift of prophecy can sometimes monopolise or jeopardise times of waiting on the Lord and giving words. So what do we do?

The truth is that we are still on a steep learning curve here, but we use both approaches 3 and 4. In other words, when we have services specifically designed for seekers I may meet beforehand with a group of prophetically gifted people and then share words received by them at the end of the service. Another approach might involve allowing only a select group of prophetic people to give prophecies during a service. This group will comprise people that I am regularly meeting with and mentoring in the prophetic – people, in other words, in whom I have confidence.

The important thing in using prophecy is to exercise *wisdom*. This is true for prophecy uttered in public worship and it is equally true for prophecy uttered in personal evangelism. Daniel not only had the ability to see visions and interpret dreams, he also had the spirit of *hokmah*, or 'wisdom'. Those who prophesy need to combine the spirit of revelation with the spirit of wisdom (see Ephesians 1:17, NIV). So ask for wisdom, and ask with faith, not unbelief. As we read in James 1:5–8:

If you need wisdom – if you want to know what God wants you to do – ask him, and he will gladly tell you. He will not resent your asking. But when you ask him, be sure that you really expect him to answer, for a doubtful mind is as unsettled as a wave of the sea that is driven and tossed by the wind. People like that should not expect to receive anything from the Lord. They can't make up their minds. They waver back and forth in everything they do.

If we ask in faith for wisdom we will receive it. As we then use wisdom in our use of prophecy we will find that there are rich results. As James goes on to say in 3:17–18:

The wisdom that comes from heaven is first of all pure. It is also peace loving, gentle at all times, and willing to yield to others. It is full of mercy and good deeds. It shows no partiality and is always sincere. And those who are peacemakers will plant seeds of peace and reap a harvest of goodness.

I am personally committed to having prophecy at all our worship meetings, though the way in which this is stewarded will vary according to the nature of the meeting. One thing I would love to see much more of is the phenomenon described by Paul in 1 Corinthians 14:24–25. I believe the church has yet to see the fullness of what Paul is describing in these verses. But I am praying very much for the day when it becomes far more normative. I want to see a day coming when there is such a high level of accuracy and authority in the prophetic that it will be said of unbelievers that 'as they listen, their secret thoughts will be laid bare, and they will fall down on their knees and worship God, declaring, "God is really here among you."'

Chapter 6

HOW GOD SPEAKS TO PEOPLE TODAY

For several years after I became a Christian (in 1977) I didn't realise that God still speaks today. I had been converted during an amazing revival at school. However, the Christians responsible for leading that work did not believe in prophecy or any other of the revelatory gifts. They firmly believed in the Bible as the Word of God, and I learned how to revere and read the Scriptures from them. But they also taught that gifts like prophecy had died out at the end of the first century and were not available today. This produced something of a lopsided spirituality in my life – a lot of emphasis on the Word, but little on the Spirit.

All that changed three years later. It was the Christmas holidays of 1980 and I was struggling with my faith. I was at that time enjoying my newfound freedom as a university undergraduate and at the same time trying to live the Christian life. As a result I was wrestling with issues of commitment and compromise.

At the height of my inner turmoil, I remember going to bed one night feeling very restless. I was at the time staying at my parents' house in Norwich Cathedral Close. I remember shutting the door and then retiring. I always shut my bedroom door as a matter of routine; my mother kept a rather large Siamese cat that used to come into my room uninvited.

I woke up very suddenly at six minutes past one in the morning. My digital alarm clock revealed the time. I was definitely awake, not sleeping.

The next moment the bedroom door flew open very quickly. Strangely, the door did not crash against the wardrobe next to it but came very suddenly to a halt a few centimetres away from it.

What happened next will remain with me for the rest of my life.

In walked a tall, white, radiant figure, about seven or eight feet in height. I looked towards the face but there were no definable features. The light was simply too bright for me to make out anything distinct. But I knew it was a face.

This being stood before me for a few seconds. I was not at all frightened. A hand reached out to me, beckoning. I heard the words, 'Follow me.' Then the figure left.

Needless to say, I was greatly impacted by this event. I told my parents the next morning. They could see that I was still in a state of shock. They were unusually receptive.

As a result of what I took to be a visit from the Lord Jesus, I decided that day to live the rest of my life completely for God and I embarked on a process leading to the ordained ministry in the Church of England. Though I have had times of weakness and wilderness since then, my heart has been wholly for the Lord.

One major consequence of that night was that I rejected the belief that God does not speak to us today. I knew already that God speaks through his written Word, the Bible. But what I did not appreciate is that Christians can have visions, visitations, revelations, dreams, words, messages and so on *today*. I had been taught that this kind of thing had died out with the death of the first apostles and that we no longer needed it because we have the Scriptures. The experience I had in my bedroom in 1980 convinced me that this view simply isn't true to the Bible or to experience. Today I believe with all of my heart that God speaks through his Word, but also by his Spirit (especially through prophecy).

So how *does* God speak to people today? In this chapter I want to examine a number of ways in which God speaks *prophetically*. In each case we will look at how he speaks to believers and to unbelievers. This is because there are essentially two types of prophetic evangelism, as I showed in chapter 1. **Type A** involves God speaking to a believer about an unbeliever. **Type B** involves God speaking directly to an unbeliever.

The list that follows is not meant to be an exhaustive one. There are many ways in which God speaks to people today. But it does give you an idea of some of the more common revelatory phenomena used by the Holy Spirit to catch both our attention and the attention of those who don't know God.

Visions and Pictures

Visions and pictures consist of revelation given visually to a person's imagination while they are awake. They involve seeing images that are presented to the eyes of one's heart. These images often communicate God's word indirectly and therefore require interpretation.

Type A

Sometimes believers will see a vision of a person or a place that God wants them to share the Gospel with. A great biblical precedent is Acts 16:9–10:

That night Paul had a vision. He saw a man from Macedonia in northern Greece, pleading with him, 'Come over here and help us.' So we decided to leave for Macedonia at once, for we could only conclude that God was calling us to preach the Good News there.

Paul had a vision of a man from Macedonia appealing to him to visit them. So Paul took that as his cue to go and evangelise that area. This is certainly an example of prophecy leading to evangelism.

People today receive visions and pictures that have an evangelistic purpose.

A friend of mine was sitting in the back of a taxi. The Lord spoke to her and she leant over and said to the man in front, 'You're not a taxi driver. You're a surgeon, and you're from the Ukraine.' The man was amazed because that is exactly what he was. He asked her how she knew and she said, 'Because Jesus told me.'

At that moment a picture dropped into her heart of a young girl with the name Anna. She shared with the man that he had a daughter called Anna. The man became very moved at this point. He had left his daughter behind in the Ukraine and missed her greatly. She was called Anastasia, Anna for short. Needless to say this revelation opened a door to the Gospel between my friend and a taxi driver she had never met!

Visions and pictures are among the most common means by which God speaks to believers about unbelievers. This has implications for the Christian arts. For years now I have been travelling with Christian painters, encouraging them to paint what they sense the Holy Spirit is giving to them in terms of visions and pictures. This has often led to believers being greatly touched and unbelievers being moved to ask questions about Jesus.

Type B

Unbelievers have prophetic visions and pictures that draw their hearts to the person of Jesus Christ. These function as *preparatio evangelica* (a Latin phrase meaning 'preparation for the Gospel').

A young Jewish man at my school in the 1970s was exposed to the claims of Christianity. For two years Christian friends witnessed to him. In the end, it was not the power of their arguments that convinced him that Jesus was the Messiah. It was receiving a vision of the empty tomb. He submitted his life to the Lord Jesus and went on to run Jews for Jesus in the UK.

In my book *Fire and Blood* (about the work of the Cross and the Spirit) I told the true story of a Cambodian village whose inhabitants had become Christians. An elderly lady in the village in Khampong Thom told how the Khmer Rouge had been about to execute them all. Some of the villagers called out to Buddha, others to other gods. But she had a vision of 'the God who hung upon a cross'. 'None but I can save you,' she heard. So she cried out to him and encouraged others to as well.

All the villagers were miraculously rescued and they gave themselves to praying to the God on a Cross. Twenty years later a Christian missionary came and shared the Gospel and they recognised instantly that the vision had been one of Jesus. Now there is a church in the village, whose existence is owed to a prophetic vision given to an unbeliever. This is an amazing example of what the theologians call 'prevenient grace' – the grace that God gives to unbelievers *before* they become Christians.

Dreams

Dreams are of great interest today. There is in fact a whole industry of dream interpretation in the UK and the US. Those who practise dream interpretation acknowledge the biblical origins of this practice. They point for example to Joseph's ability to interpret Pharaoh's dreams in the book of Genesis and Daniel's ability to interpret Nebuchadnezzar's dreams in Daniel chapters 1–4.

What then are dreams? A dream consists of a series of images that appear to our imaginations while we are asleep. Many dreams are simply the reflection of episodes and emotions from the past, especially the recent past. They spring from the subconscious mind. At other times dreams are supernatural in origin. They are used to convey messages from God. Through dreams, God can speak to believers and unbelievers alike.

The potential of dream interpretation in evangelism is huge. In an average lifespan we spend six years dreaming: that's 2,100 days spent in a world of spiritual significance, just waiting for explanation.

So how might prophetic dreams be useful in leading seekers to the Lord Jesus Christ?

Type A

Sometimes a believer may have a dream about a person that they are going to meet, with details about their lives revealed in the dream. Most commonly, however, the believer's role is more like that of Joseph and Daniel. In other words, it involves the special ability to interpret the dreams that unbelievers have.

It is interesting to note that John Paul Jackson, of Streams Ministries International, has been pioneering dream interpretation as a method of evangelism. Recently John Paul sent four thoroughly trained 'dream teams' to the Olympic Games and there were long queues of people waiting to hear the interpretation of significant dreams. The Christians on these teams saw many tears as seekers received ministry. There were a number of conversions as well.

John Paul Jackson has now started a national dream team to send to big events like the Super Bowl. This has caught the attention of the media in the US and John Paul has been on national television being interviewed about this method of outreach. You can find out about this ministry at www.streamsministries.com.

Type B

There is huge interest in dreams in UK society today. Everyone, irrespective of their age, seems to be dreaming dreams! Celia Brayfield wrote this in *The Times* newspaper on 6 March 2001:

> In a famous verse in the book of Joel, God promises to pour out his Spirit . . . when 'your old men shall dream dreams, your young men shall see visions'. These ancient and evocative words are surprisingly close to modern reality, according to a survey of a representative sample of 500 people in Britain carried out for Unmissable Ltd, a company which has set out to offer its clients the chance to make their dreams come true.
>
> A questionnaire and focus groups probed the respondents' dreams and fantasies. Among the findings were the ages at which people actually make lists of the things they dream of doing in their lives. Three people in every five have done this.
>
> The peak dreaming ages proved to be the very young

and the seriously mature. Unsurprisingly, adolescence
is the great age for making a wish list, with nearly 70%
of under-24s writing down their life's goals. . . . The
figures show that as people grow up the wish list is put
away, but at 55 it comes out again, with 64% of people in
this group keeping a list which is revised, updated and
finally used as an agenda for the rest of life.

God is using dreams to speak to those who do not yet
know his love. We have seen this in chapter 1 with
reference to Muslims. As I shared there, many Muslims
are having visions and dreams in which Jesus is
revealing himself to them as 'The Way'. But this is not
just happening to Muslims: it is happening to other
people too. Even in the secular West, people are
experiencing this sort of revelatory phenomenon.

Not long ago I was speaking to a lady called Theresa.
She is married and both she and her husband are on the
leadership team of a church that has grown to over three
thousand purely through evangelism. I found myself sitting
next to her at a supper, so I asked her how she came to
know the Lord Jesus Christ. She replied that she and her
husband had formerly been into New Age spirituality and
had run a retreat house for those wanting to explore ways
of tuning in to the supernatural dimension of life. After a
while things began to go very badly wrong. Their marriage
began to deteriorate and strange things began to occur in
their retreat house. One evening she had been upstairs in
her bedroom while a levitation class had been going on
downstairs. As that proceeded, weird and unexplainable
things started to happen in the house as furniture started to
move and loud noises were heard. Theresa was terrified.

A few weeks later she had a dream. She saw a beautiful
snowy landscape with a large barn ahead of her. The barn

looked warm and welcoming, so she walked towards it. When she entered it, however, she fell into a dark pit. As she looked up, to her horror she saw a giant spider coming down from the ceiling. All she could think of doing was to shout the name of Jesus. As she did so, the spider disappeared and she heard a voice saying, 'Theresa, I am the Way, and I am the one you're looking for.'

Theresa gave her life to Jesus, as did her husband. They shut down the retreat centre (which they now recognised as a place of danger spiritually) and are now serving in leadership in a vibrant evangelistic church – all because God spoke to Theresa in a dream!

'Open Visions'

In chapter 1 we looked at the divine appointment between Cornelius (a Gentile seeker) and Simon Peter. Cornelius has a vision in which an angel speaks to him. Peter has a 'trance' in which God shows him a vision and enters into dialogue with him:

> *The next day as Cornelius's messengers were nearing the city, Peter went up to the flat roof to pray. It was about midday, and he was hungry. But while lunch was being prepared, he fell into a trance. He saw the sky open, and something like a large sheet was let down by its four corners. In the sheet were all sorts of animals, reptiles, and birds. Then a voice said to him, 'Get up, Peter; kill and eat them' (Acts 10:9–13).*

It is all too easy to be put off by the word 'trance' in verse 10. The Greek word used by Luke here is *ekstasis*, from which we get 'ecstasy'. This is a word with very negative connotations in our culture. Its nuances range from an illicit drug to out-of-control behaviour. But in Acts 10:10 Luke intends no such negativity. In the book of Acts the word *ekstasis* is used four times. On one occasion it can be translated 'amazement' (Acts 3:10). Here, in Acts 10:10 (and in Peter's report of the same incident in Acts 11:5) it can be translated 'trance'. In Acts 22 Paul addresses the crowds, giving his testimony about how he saw Jesus on the Damascus Road, and how he was subsequently baptised by Ananias. He then goes on to report in verses 17–18:

> *One day after I returned to Jerusalem, I was praying in the Temple, and I fell into a trance. I saw a vision of Jesus saying to me, 'Hurry! Leave Jerusalem, for the people here won't believe you when you give them your testimony about me.'*

Here again, the word is *ekstasis*. Clearly, both Peter and Paul experienced occasional trance-like states.

I prefer not to use the word 'trance' because of the baggage it carries in our culture. My preferred term is 'open vision'. The difference between a vision and an open vision is simple. In a vision, the person seeing the vision is passive. It is like watching a film in which you yourself do not participate. In an 'open vision', you are active, not passive. You participate in what is going on, usually by entering into dialogue with God as he speaks with you (as Peter and Paul do). Paul's vision on the Damascus Road may well have been such an 'open vision' or trance (Acts 9:3–9). The same may be true of his visit to the third heaven described in 2 Corinthians 12:2–4.

Both believers and unbelievers may experience open visions. If these are God-inspired they will lead to seekers experiencing a revelation of Jesus Christ.

Type A

Peter in Acts 10 is the model here. He participates in an open vision that leads directly to him visiting a seeker's house and preaching the Gospel, with great effect.

With such experiences we need to be careful to proceed beyond revelation to interpretation, and from interpretation to application. The revelation in this case is very strange and obscure. Peter sees a sheet coming down from heaven with unclean creatures on it. Three times he is told to rise up, kill and eat these creatures. He struggles with obedience but eventually yields to the Lord's word: 'If God says something is acceptable, don't say it isn't' (v. 15).

Peter is subsequently unclear about the correct interpretation of this revelation. Luke reports in verse 17, 'Peter was very perplexed. What could the vision mean?' With the arrival of the three 'unclean' Gentiles from Cornelius' household Peter begins to understand. This leads to application as he goes with them to Cornelius, preaches the Gospel, and sees the whole household respond to his message and receive the gift of the Holy Spirit. All this occurs as the result of a believer experiencing an open vision. We should be prepared to let God use this form of prophetic revelation in evangelism.

Type B

There are occasions when unbelievers experience trances or 'open visions'. In the story of the pagan sorcerer Balaam (recorded in Numbers 24), it is clear that this man experienced 'trances' inspired by God. Balaam introduces his prophecy in verses 3–4 as follows:

> This is the prophecy of Balaam son of Beor, the prophecy of the

*man whose eyes see clearly, who hears the words of God, who sees
a vision from the Almighty, who falls down with eyes wide open.*

The King James Version renders the Hebrew word *naphal*
('falls down') as follows: 'He hath said, which heard the
words of God, which saw the vision of the Almighty,
falling into a trance, but having his eyes open.'

As in Balaam's time, so today unbelievers can
experience trances. A friend of mine called Graham was
recently in a pub ministering to seekers through dream
interpretation. A young woman in her twenties came to
him and started to describe a recurring nightmare in
which a murderer came into her bedroom with a knife
and attempted to stab her. This had plagued her for years.

As she was describing her dream, she went into a trance-
like state. My friend asked the Holy Spirit to give him
revelation. The Lord told him to ask the girl to look over the
shoulder of the murderer standing in the doorway. She
replied that she saw nothing. Then he asked her again. This
time she saw a pinprick of brilliant light that began to grow.
She saw a figure bathed in light standing in the door; he laid
his hand on the murderer. The murderer then fell to the floor.
She said, 'He's dead! He's gone for ever.' She then paused
and asked my friend, 'Who was that radiant figure?' He told
her that it was Jesus and she gave her life to the Lord there
and then. Today she is a committed follower of Christ.

Evidently, God can use 'open visions' not only in
addressing believers but also in appealing to the lost!

Impressions and Thoughts

This is the most common way in which God speaks to
people.

Perhaps the biggest mistake people make when it comes to the prophetic is to think that God always speaks directly and loudly. This in fact is the exception rather than the rule. God does not ordinarily call us on some heavenly telephone using an audible voice. Rather God speaks to us about unbelievers through impressions and intuitions. Over time we learn to discern when he is speaking to us, who he is speaking to us about, and what he is saying. This is a learning process. When my wife phones me unexpectedly, I know her voice without her needing to say her name. This is because of twenty years of growing intimacy through constant communication. So it is with the Lord. As we grow in intimacy with him through worship and prayer, so we learn when it is him speaking and when it is not.

Type A

How do believers receive prophetic thoughts and impressions about unbelievers?

Usually we will be with someone or will see someone and feel drawn to talk to them. Sometimes we know the person. Sometimes we don't know them but we sense there is something familiar about them. This is usually the Lord highlighting that person. Next we are suddenly aware of an impression, a thought or a piece of information that has come quite suddenly to mind. This spontaneously given snippet of knowledge usually occurs without any preceding thought processes that have any logical connection with it. Most often it comes spontaneously. All of a sudden we are aware that we have been given revelation and that we need to share it sensitively. Our hearts beat a little louder and faster as we force our way through the embarrassment barrier and begin to share.

Hopefully we are able to weave this revelation into an unforced conversation with the unbeliever or seeker in question. A relevant word awakens faith.

As an example, a John Wright tells of an experience on holiday in the West Indies:

> We were at a Barbados beachside restaurant. Across the room a middle-aged man was about to take a photograph of his wife – always a good opportunity to make an acquaintance! I leapt to my feet and offered to take the photograph of them both. The man was very appreciative. As I took the photograph, I asked the Holy Spirit what business the man was in. Into my mind came the thought, 'property'.
>
> So I said, 'I hear you are a property developer.'
>
> 'How on earth did you know that?' he asked.
>
> 'God just told me,' I replied.
>
> 'That's amazing,' he said. 'My son is a born-again Methodist and he has been trying to get me to go to church with him.'
>
> 'Well, your son's prayers have been answered and you have now had a boot in the backside in Barbados to make sure you go next time.'

Type B

There is no doubt that God speaks directly into the lives of unbelievers through impressions and thoughts. This can come in all sorts of different ways. For example, a young man – not a Christian – was watching an episode of the TV show *The Simpsons* and he saw Bart Simpson praying that God would make it possible for him not to go to school the next day. As this non-Christian man watched Bart praying, he had the strongest impression that God was talking to him about the fact that he *never* prayed. This challenged him.

The next day he was travelling on the bus to work, as he always did, and he went past a church. He saw an advertisement for a meeting with J. John. He went to it and gave his life to Jesus. All this started when he received an impression that God was talking to him while he was watching *The Simpsons*! Is anything too hard for the Lord? When it comes to prophecy, we should not limit God!

Puns and Riddles

In Jeremiah 1:11–12 we read:

> *Then the LORD said to me, 'Look, Jeremiah! What do you see?' And I replied, 'I see a branch from an almond tree.' And the LORD said, 'That's right, and it means that I am watching, and I will surely carry out my threats of punishment.'*

This is a classic example of a prophetic wordplay. Jeremiah says that he sees a *shawkade*, meaning an almond tree. God says, I will *shawkade*, or watch over, my word to perform it. Sometimes the pun is mightier than the sword!

Type A

God often speaks to me through wordplays. I was once ministering at a summer conference called New Wine. Driving my car one evening I passed a big lorry with the name of the firm emblazoned on the front, 'M.E. Heal'.

As I looked at that, I sensed the Lord saying, 'I am going to heal people with ME.' The next morning I gave that word and we prayed for people with ME. I have received two reports so far of people who were healed. That is a good example of the way God speaks through wordplay. This can happen in evangelism too.

Type B

An elderly lady called Olive, far away from God, was walking down the road outside our church. A young child, knowing that the service had already started, looked at her and shouted, 'It's very late for church.' She interpreted the word 'late' not only as 'late in time' but 'late in age'. Feeling that she might not have much time left in her life, Olive came to church and gave her life to the Lord Jesus Christ. God spoke a prophetic word to Olive through an unintended pun uttered by a child!

Messages from God

God speaks by laying a message on a believer's heart. This can be anything from a sentence to a page in length. Unbelievers can receive these as well. Very rarely they will come with the audible voice of God. Most often they are inaudible and received by the ears of the heart.

Type A

Messages come in the form of a sense of God saying or asking something. John Wright reports:

Walking down Knightsbridge, London, a little early for a

business appointment, I passed a young man in his late twenties sitting in a shop doorway, begging. I was somewhat shocked. He looked young and fit and surely could have found a job. I grumbled to God about the younger generation needing to get off their backsides. As the thought came into my mind, I quickly repented of my judgemental thoughts. Returning to the young man, I sat down beside him and asked him his name.

'Mark,' he said.

'God told me to come back and tell you that he loves you,' I said.

Then I discovered the wonder of it all when I heard Mark reply:

'I am a backslidden Christian. You are the third person today who has stopped to tell me the same thing!'

Type B

In 1977 I was walking down Kingsgate Street, Winchester, at 11 o'clock at night and I distinctly sensed a voice within my heart saying the words, 'Mark Stibbe, if you died tonight, where would you stand before the judgement seat of God?' That message from God (in the form of a question) put holy fear into my heart and I ran to a Christian's house, whereupon I submitted the whole of my life to Jesus Christ.

Scriptures

Sometimes believers are moved by the Holy Spirit to share a verse of Scripture with a seeker, one that seems to speak right into their situation at that moment. At other times, seekers can find Bible verses that speak directly to their hearts, leading to a strong sense that God is speaking to them personally.

Type A

Here is a typical example of what I mean. A friend of mine writes:

> One November morning, on the train to London, I had finished breakfast and was reading the Bible when an elegantly dressed lady got on to the train, sat down in the seat across the gangway and began to order her meal. As she spoke to the waiter, the Holy Spirit spoke to me, 'Give her a Psalm for breakfast.'
>
> It was brief and to the point and foolish. It was as if I was being asked to pass the marmalade! 'Lord, I can't do that, there is a great gangway fixed between us. If I accost her with a Bible she will send for the guard and have me put off the train. I shall miss my appointment in London!'
>
> So I argued, but to no avail. Eventually I gave up and asked in exasperation what Psalm was on the menu this morning. It was Psalm 62, a Psalm of encouragement, which starts: 'For God alone my soul waits in silence; from him comes my salvation. He only is my rock and my salvation, my fortress; I shall not be greatly moved.'
>
> With the waiter gone I offered the Bible, open at Psalm 62, to the lady.
>
> 'Excuse me, would you like a Psalm for breakfast?'
>
> She jumped with astonishment but after a momentary pause while she surveyed the source of this unexpected interruption to her breakfast, she accepted the Bible. A few moments later the lady returned the Bible with tears in her eyes.
>
> 'That was just what I needed to hear. I have been

through a terrible time recently and am just off on holiday to recover. That was God speaking to me. I am a Roman Catholic.'

Using Bible verses is a potent form of sharing God's word. The Bible is the Word of God. When a seeker hears the written Word applied to them personally, the Holy Spirit quickens that word in their hearts so that they really feel that God is speaking to them directly.

The book of Psalms is a great resource for prophetic evangelism. John Paul Jackson, whom I wrote about in the section on dreams, takes teams of mature prophetic evangelists to psychic fairs. They set up a stall advertised as Psalm Reading. They have found that many New Age people have come to know Jesus Christ through having a Psalm prophetically selected and prayerfully read over them.

Type B

Many seekers read the Bible. Perhaps the classic biblical precedent is the Ethiopian eunuch who is reading from Isaiah 53 when Philip connects with him (Acts 8:26–40). The Ethiopian is intrigued by a passage from God's Word. He feels this is directly relevant to him. Philip, operating as a prophetic evangelist here, leads him to the Lord and baptises him.

There have been countless stories of this kind of thing in church history. The conversion of Augustine is a classic example. He was far away from God, living a self-indulgent, hedonistic life. One day, resting in a garden, he heard a child saying, 'Take up and read.' He took up a Bible and read verses from Romans 13:11–14 that proved utterly life-changing for him.

The Varieties of Prophetic Experience

There is no one way that God speaks prophetically, either to believers or unbelievers. In prophetic evangelism, we need to be open to the full range of possibilities, from the use of visions to the use of Bible verses. We must not limit God. He can speak in any way he decides.

In Numbers 12:6–8 God speaks to his people about prophecy. He contrasts the way he speaks with prophets with the way he speaks with Moses. With the former he uses revelatory phenomena like visions, dreams and riddles. These convey his thoughts indirectly. With Moses he speaks directly and plainly:

> *Listen to my words: 'When a prophet of the LORD is among you, I reveal myself to him in visions, I speak to him in dreams. But this is not true of my servant Moses; he is faithful in all my house. With him I speak face to face, clearly and not in riddles; he sees the form of the LORD' (NIV).*

God uses visions, dreams, 'open visions', impressions and thoughts, puns and riddles, messages, Scriptures and other means to get people's attention today. He may use divine or angelic visitations and other means in addition to these. The key thing is to be open to receiving prophetic revelation and then, when it comes, to weigh and test what one receives. It is to the vital matter of distinguishing between true and false revelation that we must now turn in the next chapter. With the current popularity of psychic and occult means of knowing secret thoughts and predicting the future, this is of paramount importance.

Chapter 7

THE NEED TO EXERCISE DISCERNMENT

One of the saddest things I have ever seen was a thriving church in Norway torn apart by spiritual deception.

This happened in the 1990s when the senior pastor of the church – a godly man who had been praying for revival in Norway for years – was introduced to some apparent new converts out of the New Age movement. The main figure, whom I will call Lars, was an extremely powerful personality. He had the ability to read people's lives with great accuracy and he had allegedly led a group of New Agers to Christ using this 'gift'. The group grew and the senior pastor was drawn in when Lars claimed God had told him to invite him.

What happened next was very tragic. In spite of what looked like good beginnings – more New Agers coming to Christ through this core group – there were signs of something not quite right. The claims of conversions (numbering into the thousands) could not be substantiated. Questions were asked about the nature of Lars' gift. Was it really a prophetic gift or was it a psychic or even a demonic counterfeit?

Eventually the movement went completely off the rails. A woman even more powerful than Lars joined the group. She started to claim that the members didn't need to read the Bible. She argued that you could hear the Father for yourself, with 100 per cent accuracy. The Bible is a good book, but why read that when you can go directly to the author?

Inevitably this led to unbiblical views. The woman in question (I'll call her Elizabeth) began to teach that a man could have more than one wife. He could have the wife he had married but he could also have what she called a 'soul wife' – a spiritual mate in addition to his actual mate. No one thought to question this. Lars and Elizabeth seemed to have a direct line to God. How could anyone dare question them?

I was brought in to the picture as part of a small international team of theologians to look at the teaching of this group. I concluded, along with my colleagues, that the two main players were false prophets and that they were seducing people with false teaching. The fruits of this movement bore this out. Tragically, the senior pastor's marriage ended. The church he was leading – one of the largest churches in Norway – was divided and almost destroyed in the process. Considerable damage was done in relation to the gift and ministry of prophecy in Norway and scepticism set in concerning revival. All in all, it was a very painful lesson about the power of deception and the need for discernment. It was a shame that this lesson had to be learned the hard way.

The Dangers of Deception

I start this chapter with that tale because there is a great need to be discerning when it comes to the matter of using prophecy in evangelism. Throughout church history there have been powerful people who have claimed to hear what God is saying and who have secured significant followings. In some cases this has led to gross deception and great disasters. These 'charismatic' leaders and their followers almost inevitably end up destroying themselves and others. The damage done to the cause of Christ can sometimes be great.

I say this because even the most spiritual people in the church can be deceived. The senior pastor of the church in Norway was a fine man. I knew him. He was a passionate follower of the Lord Jesus Christ. He was a very able leader (who had led the church into significant growth). He was absolutely sold out for revival in Norway. He was also a gifted Bible teacher and a man who moved in the gifts of the Spirit. In every respect he was a good leader who believed in the marriage of the Word and the Spirit. Yet he was deceived. When I tell you that his wife had been converted from a New Age background, that she had discerned that something was very wrong in Lars and his group, and that she had warned her husband, the situation appears even more incredible.

How could the pastor have been so taken in? The answer is not hard to find. The truth is, deception is very powerful. The lethal thing about deception is its close proximity to truth. For a thing to have the power to deceive, it must look as close to the real thing as possible without being itself real. Take banknotes as an example. Counterfeit notes would not deceive anyone unless they were as close as possible to real banknotes. So it is with spiritual things. The devil is a master counterfeiter. When he attempts to deceive people he does so by imitating God's work. The devil is incapable of either originality or creativity. He is a forger, a copier, a dissembler. Therefore he works by producing demonic imitations that are close to God's original design. As I sometimes put it, 'Deception wouldn't be so deceptive if it wasn't so close to truth.' Or, as Paul puts it in 2 Corinthians, speaking about the false teachers in Corinth:

> *These people are false apostles. They have fooled you by disguising themselves as apostles of Christ. But I am not surprised! Even Satan can disguise himself as an angel of light. So it is no wonder his servants can also do it by pretending to be godly ministers. In the end they will get every bit of punishment their wicked deeds deserve (2 Cor. 11:13–15).*

The dangers of deception are therefore very real, especially in the area of prophecy. The person who claims to hear what God is saying is more vulnerable to the charge of subjectivism than anyone. The person who wants to grow in the prophetic needs to learn what is true and what is false prophecy. This is really important because there is a lot of false prophecy in the world today. Many people are claiming to be able to read other people's lives and to tell their futures. Lars, the man at the centre of the Norway controversy, had this ability. I remember sitting with him and hearing him tell me about my wife and four children (none of whom he knew). It was powerful, yet it made me feel uneasy. It was so close to real prophecy, yet it was not.

Realising the dangers, many people in the church say, 'Well, if the road's that perilous, at least potentially, I'd rather not travel on it.' But this would be a mistake. Yes, Jesus warns us about the dangers of deception. He says in Matthew 24:

> *Don't let anyone mislead you. For many will come in my name, saying, 'I am the Messiah.' They will lead many astray (v. 4–5).*

> *And many false prophets will appear and will lead many people astray (v. 11).*

> *For false messiahs and false prophets will rise up and perform great miraculous signs and wonders so as to deceive, if possible, even God's chosen ones. See, I have warned you (vv. 24–25).*

Yes, there is the danger of deception, and Jesus warns us ahead of time about that. At the same time, nowhere in the Bible is there any suggestion that we should reject the prophetic because of that. Rather, we are encouraged to regard prophecy as something positive and we are to handle the gift in a wise way. As Paul writes in 1 Thessalonians 5:19–22:

> *Do not stifle the Holy Spirit. Do not scoff at prophecies, but test everything that is said. Hold on to what is good. Keep away from every kind of evil.*

We must be careful not to cultivate a negative attitude towards prophecy. To put it another way, *we must not become so put off by the devil's ability to deceive that we forget the Lord's ability to bless.*

The Gift of Discernment

A responsible use of prophecy in evangelism means that we put a strong emphasis on exercising discernment. In the list of the spiritual gifts in 1 Corinthians 12:9–10, the gift of discernment is mentioned right after the gift of prophecy. The New Living Translation says of the Holy Spirit, 'He gives someone else the ability to know whether it is really the Spirit of God or another spirit that is speaking' (v. 10).

This is a good translation of the original Greek, which literally means 'the ability to judge between spirits'. When it comes to what looks like a prophetic utterance, there are three possible sources: the Holy Spirit, our human spirits, and an unholy spirit (a spirit of deception). The gift of discernment is vital for deciding which of these three lies behind a purported prophecy.

The gift of discernment is the special ability to discern whether the human spirit, the Holy Spirit, or an evil spirit is at work behind a particular phenomenon.

Of course, we must not assume that all our words are divinely inspired! In fact it is very instructive to watch what happens with Simon Peter in Matthew 16. As he speaks, he utters words that have a human origin, words that are clearly divine in origin, and words that are demonically inspired – all within the space of a few minutes. In his conversation with Jesus at Caesarea Philippi, Peter begins by joining others in reporting what human beings are saying about Jesus:

> *When Jesus came to the region of Caesarea Philippi, he asked his disciples, 'Who do people say that the Son of Man is?' 'Well,' they replied, 'some say John the Baptist, some say Elijah, and others say Jeremiah or one of the other prophets' (Mt. 16:13–14).*

In the next breath we see Peter moving from human thoughts to divinely inspired thoughts:

> *Then he asked them, 'Who do you say I am?' Simon Peter answered, 'You are the Messiah, the Son of the living God.' Jesus replied, 'You are blessed, Simon son of John, because my Father in heaven has revealed this to you. You did not learn this from any human being. Now I say to you that you are Peter, and upon this rock I will build my church, and all the powers of hell will not conquer it. And I will give you the keys of the Kingdom of Heaven. Whatever you lock on earth will be locked in heaven, and whatever you open on earth will be opened in heaven.' Then he sternly warned them not to tell anyone that he was the Messiah (Mt. 16:15–20).*

From words that are inspired by the Father, poor old

Peter moves immediately to words inspired by the devil!

> *From then on Jesus began to tell his disciples plainly that he had to go to Jerusalem, and he told them what would happen to him there. He would suffer at the hands of the leaders and the leading priests and the teachers of religious law. He would be killed, and he would be raised on the third day. But Peter took him aside and began to reprimand him. 'Heaven forbid, Lord,' he said. 'This will never happen to you!' Jesus turned to Peter and said, 'Get away from me, Satan! You are a dangerous trap to me' (Mt. 16:21–23).*

Peter's thinking exhibits three different sources in the space of a few minutes! During one conversation with Jesus his words clearly exhibit a human, then a prophetic, then a demonic source. If Peter could be caught out like this, we should exercise caution. Of course, we have the Holy Spirit within us today, while Peter was here speaking before Pentecost. But this should not give us any licence to be complacent. Discernment is called for in the prophetic.

Discernment on the Streets

The early church exercised discernment not only in the church but also in the world. In New Testament times, the first Christians were confronted by counterfeits of true prophecy as they took the Gospel out onto the streets. Within their multi-faith context they came across occult perversions of the prophetic. Some of these promised the ability to read people's lives and tell people's futures. These looked very similar to genuine prophecy, so the need to be discerning became paramount.

Take, for example, the incident described by Luke in Acts 16:16–18. Paul and Silas are in the city of Philippi and they experience the following incident:

> *One day as we were going down to the place of prayer, we met a demon-possessed slave girl. She was a fortune-teller who earned a lot of money for her masters. She followed along behind us shouting, 'These men are servants of the Most High God, and they have come to tell you how to be saved.' This went on day after day until Paul got so exasperated that he turned and spoke to the demon within her. 'I command you in the name of Jesus Christ to come out of her,' he said. And instantly it left her.*

The interesting thing about this story is the fact that the woman who had an evil spirit was actually proclaiming the truth. She was giving Paul and Silas free publicity, declaring that they were showing the path to salvation. Far from speaking under the anointing for prophecy, however, the slave-girl was actually motivated by a demon. Luke describes this demon as 'a spirit of divination', or literally, 'a python spirit'. The word 'python' is significant because the Greek god of wisdom was Apollo, and his symbol was a python. The most famous place for fortune-telling was the Oracle at Delphi, where the priestess (the Pythia) acted as the prophet of Apollo.

When Luke describes the slave-girl's source of inspiration as 'a python spirit' he is identifying that spirit with the same force that inspired the Pythian priestess at Delphi. This spirit had possessed the slave-girl to such a degree that she could speak into people's lives and tell their future. In fact, she was so successful at this that her masters had made a lucrative business out of her.

For many days Paul and Silas allowed this girl to follow them around the city wherever they went. As she did so she would shout out (the word can mean 'shrieked') who they were and what they were doing. Her insight was absolutely correct. Paul and Silas were servants of the Most High God and they had come to Philippi to preach the way of salvation. But Paul, after a while, became troubled. Luke does not tell us how or why. He merely used a word that can be translated 'grieved'. Paul became uneasy and even anxious about the source of the girl's motivation. Having tolerated it for days, Paul suddenly turns round and commands the spirit inside the girl to come out, which it duly does at that very hour.

Why did Paul take so long ('many days') before dealing with this spirit? It may be that he was not bothered by it to begin with. It may be that he felt compassion for the girl. It may be that he had anticipated the negative consequences of dealing with the spirit, and wanted to minister to as many people as possible before being arrested.

The most probable cause of this delay was that Paul was exercising the gift of discernment (about which he himself wrote in 1 Corinthians 12:10). Paul was allowing time to test and evaluate the spirit operating in the slave-girl's life. The spirit of divination in the girl's life was leading her to declare true insights. This made it highly deceptive. Paul waited until he felt grieved in his spirit before delivering the girl of what was the source of her spiritual slavery. Sometimes that is all we are going to have as well. Nothing more objective than what is sometimes called 'a shiver in the liver'. Discernment is therefore a challenge. The devil rarely makes it obvious that he is at work when it comes to the demonic counterfeits of true prophecy.

Divination, the Devil's Counterfeit

The most dangerous counterfeit of prophecy – both in Paul's time and our own – is divination.

Divination in the first century was the art of acquiring secret knowledge, especially knowledge relating to the future. There were essentially two main ways of acquiring this secret knowledge. There was first of all the **natural divination** that depended on humanly learned skills such as interpreting signs. The second way was more supernatural than natural and relied on the possession of a spirit or a deity. This second method was known as **supernatural divination**. Here the person receiving the secret knowledge would often go into a trance-like dream, or into a state of ecstasy.

What Paul and Silas encountered in Philippi was the second form of divination. In other words, the girl who was able to tell people's fortunes was not using artificial but inspirational divination. The evidence for this is everywhere in the text. In the Greek culture of Paul's day, the diviner who obtained their knowledge from spirits was known as a *mantis* and their art was known as *mantike*. In Acts 16:16 the woman is said to have made her employers rich through her fortune-telling. The word translated fortune-telling is the verb *manteuomai*, which is closely related to *mantis* and *mantike*. She was clearly using **supernatural divination**.

That she had the supernatural rather than the natural kind of divination is further suggested by the fact that she goes round shouting out her knowledge about Paul's message. As I wrote earlier, the word 'shouted' can also be translated 'screamed' or 'shrieked'. Why should that be important? This kind of frenzied behaviour was common in inspirational or supernatural divination in the ancient world. The Pythian priestess at Delphi used to behave in this way. A contemporary of Luke's, the historian Lucan (AD 39–65), described how the Pythia at Delphi frantically careered around the cave where the oracles were delivered, scattering the furniture in all directions, and uttering loud cries and wails (*De Bello Civili* 5.169–94).

From the earliest days of Christianity there has therefore been a counterfeit of prophecy known as divination. On the surface of it, the two look very similar. In both prophecy and divination, secret spiritual knowledge is disclosed, often about the future. But one big difference is that the source of prophecy is the Holy Spirit while the source of divination is an unholy spirit. Though it may not be immediately obvious which we are witnessing in certain situations, Paul's example reveals that a sense of uneasiness is often a clue and that time will tell. When an unholy spirit of divination is at work in a person, it needs to be discerned and the person needs to be delivered.

Believers who want to grow in the prophetic need to be alert to the differences between prophecy and divination. The Bible condemns divination but encourages prophecy. Passages like Deuteronomy 18:9–12 are unequivocal about occult practices like divination, and make no distinction between the supernatural and natural versions:

> *When you arrive in the land the LORD your God is giving you, be very careful not to imitate the detestable customs of the nations living there. For example, never sacrifice your son or daughter as a burnt offering. And do not let your people practise fortune-telling or sorcery, or allow them to interpret omens, or engage in witchcraft, or cast spells, or function as mediums or psychics, or call forth the spirits of the dead. Anyone who does these things is an object of horror and disgust to the LORD.*

Divination – whether supernatural/inspirational or natural/artificial – is clearly described here as hateful in the eyes of the Lord. There is no beating about the bush here. Having said that, we should note that the *practice* of divination is described as detestable, not the *person*. When Paul turns to address the fortune-teller in Philippi, he does not speak sternly to the person but to the spirit. When we have a situation where someone is into divination rather than prophecy, we must be careful to follow Paul's example and hate the demon, not the person.

Distinguishing Between Prophecy and Divination

So how do we tell the difference between prophecy and its demonic counterfeit?

Here we need to remember that the gift of discernment is just that, a *gift*. It is a special ability given by the Holy Spirit. This ability enables a believer to make a right judgement about the spirit motivating a word or an action.

Given that discernment in this sense is an anointing of the Holy Spirit, we should understand that the ability to distinguish between the true and the false is going to be first and foremost more an intuitive than a logical matter. This will be far too subjective for many people, but there's no avoiding it. When Paul eventually discerned what was going on in the slave-girl's life it was because he felt upset, unsettled and even disturbed. He just knew the girl was demonised. To be sure, he may have consulted with Silas, prayed with him, and even discussed some more objective criteria. But in the final analysis, all Luke points to is the way Paul felt. He felt 'grieved'.

Those gifted in the area of discernment will often have an uneasy sense that something is not quite right about the source of a particular utterance, action, situation or object. This is particularly true when divination is at work. In the more supernatural forms of divination it should become clear to someone operating in the gift of discernment that demonic spirits are involved. Sooner or later this should register on the spiritual radar of any believer who is reasonably sensitive. A deep sense of unease will set in. In the natural types of divination it may be less obvious whether there are demonic forces at work. Discernment may take longer here, but it is still called for.

Bishop David Pytches lists the contemporary methods of divination in his excellent handbook entitled *Prophecy in the Local Church*. He defines the divination forbidden in Scripture as 'the unveiling of hidden (occult) and forbidden knowledge from the past, present and future'. He includes the following:

Arithmancy (from numbers)
Coffee-grout reading
Horoscopy (from stars)
Geomancy (from dots)
Cartomancy (from cards)
Crystallomancy (crystal gazing)
Capromancy (smoke reading)
Dice reading
Liver reading
Lead pouring
Pyromancy (fire reading)
Selenomancy (moon divination)
Sun divination
Sleep reading
Tephromancy (ash reading)
Tea leaves
Pendulums
White of egg in drinking glass
Bird formation in flight

Whether these methods are examples of supernatural or natural divination (or a mixture of the two), the Bible is clear: God's people are to having nothing to do with them. They are 'detestable' to the Lord.

In addition to the more subjective, intuitive response to divinatory phenomena it is also helpful to use some objective tests. There are major differences between the spirit of prophecy (the true) and the spirit of divination (the false). When we become aware of these differences we can judge better what we are dealing with.

So, first of all, prophecy comes from God whereas divination comes from the devil. Their sources are different.

Secondly, prophecy, if it is genuine, will be entirely consistent with what the Bible teaches. Divination will not be biblical.

Thirdly, genuine prophecy points people to Jesus, the Jesus who was born of a virgin, lived in Israel, died on a cross, rose from the dead, is seated in glory, and will return on the Last Day. Divination does *not* do this! It leads people *away* from Jesus or to a different Jesus.

Fourthly, genuine prophecy is non-manipulative, whereas divination is manipulative and controlling.

Fifthly, prophecy results in holy fear. Divination results in unholy fear. Prophecy exposes the secrets of the heart and results in the recipient acknowledging that God knows their thoughts. This in turn leads to comfort or conviction. With divination fear is often released. A person becomes locked into a fatalistic view of what is coming. When divination doesn't evoke unholy fear, it brings false comfort, promising peace where there is no peace.

Sixthly, genuine prophecy is given freely. It is a gift freely given to the one who is speaking. That person then freely gives away what the Lord has given. With divination it is altogether different. Often the one doing the divining has a financial incentive and may, like the slave-girl in Acts 16, be tied into money motives.

Seventhly, genuine prophecy bears good fruit in a person's life, leading to greater dependence upon God and closeness to Jesus (Mt. 7:15–20). Divination produces bad fruit in the form of dependency upon the diviner and/or self-gratification.

So there are some more objective tests that can be used. The main differences between prophecy and divination can be summarised thus:

Prophecy	Divination
Comes from God	Is demonic
Is consistent with Scripture	Is non-biblical or unbiblical
Points to Jesus	Does not point to Jesus
Is non-manipulative	Is manipulative, controlling
Causes holy fear and/or godly comfort	Causes unholy fear and/or false comfort
Is given freely	Often has to be paid for
Bears good fruit	Bears bad fruit

By Their Fruits

Perhaps the most important criterion for discerning the true from the false is what I have elsewhere called 'the criterion of consequence'. It is from the results of a word of revelation that we get the clearest indication of whether something is truly prophetic or is psychic or demonic.

Jesus made this abundantly clear in his sermon on the mount. In Matthew 7:15–20 he used the metaphor of a tree when talking about true and false prophets. A true prophet is like a good or healthy tree and produces good fruit. A false prophet is like a bad or unhealthy tree, yielding bad fruit. Though a prophet may appear to be and say all the right things, it is only the fruit of their words that really reveals the source of their motivation and inspiration:

> *Beware of false prophets who come disguised as harmless sheep, but are really wolves that will tear you apart. You can detect them by the way they act, just as you can identify a tree by its fruit. You don't pick grapes from thorn bushes, or figs from thistles. A healthy tree produces good fruit, and an unhealthy tree produces bad fruit. A good tree can't produce bad fruit, and a bad tree can't produce good fruit. So every tree that does not produce good fruit is chopped down and thrown into the fire. Yes, the way to identify a tree or a person is by the kind of fruit that is produced (Mt. 7:15–20).*

I have a friend called Sharon Stone (not the film star!) who teaches and ministers in the area of prophecy. She operates in the UK. Sharon has also been teaching about prophetic evangelism for some years now. In her teacher's manual on what she calls 'apostolic prophetic evangelism' she tells many true stories of how she has prophesied into the lives of unbelievers. In at least some of these testimonies we get to see the fruit of these prophetic words in the lives of the people who receive them. Take the following as an example. Sharon writes:

> One afternoon as I was in a supermarket shopping, the Holy Spirit began to speak to me about a young woman in the front of the checkout queue. He told me that the young

woman's husband was beating her. At first I began to look for physical signs that would validate this word. I looked for a wedding ring on the woman's hand and bruises but saw neither. I knew I had to act upon the word but was uncertain as to what I should do. Feeling impressed to talk with the young woman, I took a deep breath, moved out of the queue and placed myself next to her. I began to talk to her, saying, 'I am a Christian and I believe God still speaks today. He has told me that your husband is beating you.'

The young woman began to cry, confessing the truth of the word. I paid for both sets of shopping produce. Out in the car park we continued to talk and the young woman gave her heart to the Lord. Later the woman's husband also gave his heart to the Lord. In the weeks and months that followed I helped the couple grow in their relationship with God and each other. Their dysfunctional relationship was on the way to being healed as they learned how to love one another and walk in the ways of God.

After a while I lost touch with the couple.

Several years later, at a conference where I was speaking, a woman approached me and began to talk.

'You may not remember me,' the woman said. 'I was the young girl you led to the Lord years ago in the supermarket car park.'

I replied, 'I do remember. How are you? What are you doing now?'

The woman shared, 'My husband and I live in the area and we are pastors of a church not far from here.'

This is one of the most powerful testimonies of prophetic evangelism I have come across. Those who practise prophetic evangelism sometimes don't see the results of the words they share. In this episode Sharon is given the privilege of actually seeing the fruit: two people converted, a marriage healed, and a couple released into full-time church leadership. I would call that good fruit!

Imitations of Prophetic Evangelism

Perhaps the main reason why we need to exercise discernment in the area of prophetic evangelism is that the devil is already counterfeiting this vital Kingdom ministry. He is producing demonic counterfeits that look close enough to the real thing to deceive people, even Christians.

A housewife in my congregation sent me a very revealing e-mail about something that had just happened to her husband, who works in finance in the city of London. The message was dated 18 October 2002. This is what she wrote:

Dear Mark,

Mike has just rung me from the City to say that a man in the street approached him and said he was a 'yogi man'. He showed him a picture of Jesus, said he had just had a revelation from God for Mike, and spoke words into his life. These were extremely accurate to the point of detail (e.g. you have five kids). The man asked Mike if he prayed, and then said he would pray for Mike for thirty-three days. To which Mike replied, well I'll pray for you.

I think this is important because, as the climate for spiritual revelation from God heats up, there are other 'religions' out there that are going to be sensing that and may speak false words into people's lives, or certainly words that are not necessarily from Jesus.

What do you think?

I think it suggests that the devil is already counterfeiting prophetic evangelism. Why is he doing this? The first reason is because he wants to deceive unbelievers. With a pervasive uncertainty and even fear about the future in today's culture, unbelievers are extremely vulnerable. Already there are people out on the streets and in the work place using divination to lure people into false religions through false prophecy. Divination provides just enough true insight to get people hooked. Once hooked, they are easily manipulated.

The second reason is because the devil wants to immobilise believers. Producing counterfeits is his way of discouraging believers from using prophecy in evangelism.

In Exodus 7:10–12 we read how God commands Moses and Aaron to perform a miracle before Pharaoh. Moses is told to throw down his staff, that his staff will become a snake, and that this sign will cause the ruler to wonder. This is what happens:

> *So Moses and Aaron went to see Pharaoh, and they performed the miracle just as the LORD had told them. Aaron threw down his staff before Pharaoh and his court, and it became a snake. Then Pharaoh called in his wise men and magicians, and they did the same thing with their secret arts. Their staffs became snakes, too! But then Aaron's snake swallowed up their snakes.*

Notice how the court magicians immediately produced a counterfeit. This is in one sense encouraging. It shows that God knows very well that the enemy mimics what he wants to do. The most encouraging thing of all, however, is that Aaron's snake devours the other snakes. While counterfeits appear, the *true* triumphs over the false.

The counterfeit of prophetic evangelism is already appearing. There is accordingly a great need for discernment as we use the gift of prophecy with unbelievers. In the prophetic words we give to unbelievers we must be extremely careful not to mix our spirits. We must keep the emphasis on Jesus. We must be biblical. We must be loving, not manipulative, and we must look for good fruit from what we share.

When we meet counterfeits of prophetic evangelism, we must ask the Holy Spirit for discernment – for that witness in our spirits about the source of what we observe. Even when a person purports to be drawing attention to Jesus, as in the case of the yogi man, we must ask, 'Which Jesus?' There are many different views of Jesus today. The New Age movement is particularly clever at talking about Jesus so as to deceive people. But it is not the Jesus of the Bible.

We are on the Winning Side!

We should be very aware that the Bible warns us about precisely this. In 1 John 4:1–3 we read:

Dear friends, do not believe everyone who claims to speak by the Spirit. You must test them to see if the spirit they have comes from God. For there are many false prophets in the world. This is the way to find out if they have the Spirit of God: If a prophet acknowledges that Jesus Christ became a human being, that person has the Spirit of God. If a prophet does not acknowledge Jesus, that person is not from God. Such a person has the spirit of the Antichrist. You have heard that he is going to come into the world, and he is already here.

At the same time we must not adopt a defeatist attitude. The genuine will swallow up the false. Miracle will triumph over magic. Remember what John says in the next verse:

> *But you belong to God, my dear children. You have already won your fight with these false prophets, because the Spirit who lives in you is greater than the spirit who lives in the world.*

Sharon Stone, whom I mentioned a short while ago, gives a graphic example of the truth of the words, 'You have already won your fight with these false prophets'. She tells how she was ministering at a conference in Asia. At the end of that conference she was invited to the home of a Christian family for a traditional Asian dinner. When she got there she realised that extended family members also lived with the family and that several of these were Buddhists, not Christians. One particularly antagonistic family member was the grandmother.

After dinner the Christian members of the family asked Sharon to minister to everyone present, including the grandmother. They told Sharon not to worry about the grandmother's reaction because she was used to hearing the Buddhist priests prophesying.

Out of deference, Sharon was asked to begin by praying for the hostile grandmother. Sharon asked the Lord for a key to open this elderly woman's heart. She began to prophesy over the old woman and said, 'And the Lord says, "Daughter, I was with you even through the hardship of your life."' As Sharon heard those words come out of her mouth she said to the Lord, 'Oh God, you have to do better than this!' But the next thing the Lord said was, 'Daughter, I was with you even when you had to give away your son.'

Before Sharon could say any more a great conversation broke out among the people present. Sharon was told that many years before, the grandmother's husband had been killed in battle. At that time the grandmother had had two daughters and was pregnant with a third child. That third child turned out to be a son. Because of her husband's death, and her consequent poverty, she had had to give away the son to her brother to raise. Sharon's prophetic word exposed this secret and revealed to the young couple hosting the meal that their cousin was really their brother! More than that, it revealed to the grandmother that Jesus is alive and that what Sharon had to offer was genuine, while what the Buddhist priests were into was not. The grandmother said to Sharon, 'Your God knows me.' Then she added, 'What can I do to get to know your God?'

Truly, we are on the winning side! If God be for us, who can be against us?

Chapter 8

WHEN PROPHECY AND HEALING MEET

One of the most encouraging conferences I have led on prophetic evangelism was in the city of Bergen in western Norway. We had a good start to the weekend on the Friday evening. After the teaching, we had a time of waiting on God for prophetic words for delegates at the conference. As a number of us stood at the front listening, the Lord began to reveal things that greatly encouraged those who received them. Clearly there was a strong anointing for prophetic ministry.

On the Saturday morning, after a bit more teaching, the delegates formed into small groups so that everyone in the conference could both receive and give prophecies. That also proved to be encouraging. Then, in the afternoon, we split into two groups. Some of the delegates went off into the city in pairs, to ask God to give them opportunities to practise using prophecy in evangelism. Others stayed behind to be led in intercessory prayer for the teams going out.

I decided on this particular occasion that I was feeling a bit rusty and so I went out with a team member called Graham. We had a couple of appointments with seekers while walking the crowded streets of Bergen. Then, at 5 o'clock in the afternoon, we decided to walk up a side street. There was no one in sight but we still felt it right to go there. As we went up the street the only person we saw was a young woman in her mid-twenties with a mobile telephone.

She was talking to someone so we didn't think to engage her in conversation. Instead, we went into an art gallery just next to where she was and looked at the exhibits. None of the items really caught our attention except a painting of Mary and Jesus that was hanging on the wall.

We left the art gallery and started to walk up the hill, resolving to go and find a restaurant. But as we walked we both felt it right to turn round again. We came down the hill where the art gallery was situated. The young woman was no longer on the street and there was no one around. As we passed the gallery we both knew without saying a word that we were to go in, so we did.

In the middle of the main exhibit room was the young woman. I just knew I had to talk with her. So I went up to her and introduced myself and Graham, explaining that we were from England. She said that she ran the gallery. I expressed my admiration for the painting of Jesus and Mary that she was actually looking at as we spoke. I then went on to tell her that we were in the process of refurbishing our church and that I was looking for a painting, but not of Jesus and Mary. I began to describe the picture I was after – a picture of the prodigal son returning to his father and the father embracing him, holding him close in his arms of love. Essentially, I used this picture to tell the parable!

As I did so I could see that the young woman was deeply moved. I asked her if she was familiar with that story. She said no, that she was not a Christian or a churchgoer. I pressed in all the same and asked her whether the picture I had just described spoke to her in any way. She said yes. This is a summary of what she went on to add: 'What you have described does speak to me. It tells me that my two little brothers are in heaven in God's arms. You see, my brothers and I have a very rare illness. The boys died from it. I am a carrier. It is incurable. Both my brothers died when they were little and I have never really got over it. But your picture suggests to me that maybe there is a heaven, and maybe God is like that father who has welcomed them home.'

As she said this, I could feel my heart breaking. I knew that I was going to cry, so I asked Graham to minister to her by sharing a word from God. Before he did that, I gently explained that we believe that God still speaks to people today. Graham then shared some beautiful words of comfort to the woman's heart. When he finished I turned to her and told her that we pray for people to receive healing in our church, and that many times people get well when we pray for them with the laying on of hands. I asked if we could pray for her. She was very receptive, so we invited the Holy Spirit to come.

And he did! As soon as we invited him, the young woman was clearly touched. Her hands started shaking, her eyelids started fluttering. She felt heat going into her body. She knew nothing about these kind of phenomena, so there was absolutely no chance of suggestion. After about two minutes of praying for her to be healed, and for the generational disease to be stopped, I asked her how she felt. She said she felt *released*!

It was a wonderful moment. Standing in the middle of the art gallery, in the presence of the Lord Jesus, with a seeker so obviously touched by the power of God. We talked to her about Jesus, and told her about some churches in the city that she should now think of trying. We left rejoicing and returned to the conference.

This is not the end of the story. When we shared our testimony with all the others that evening, the intercessors who had stayed behind became very excited.

'What time was it when you went up that side street?' asked the leader.

'Five o'clock,' we replied.

'That's amazing,' said the prayer leader. 'At 5 o'clock one of the intercessors had a vision of the Holy Spirit moving like a mighty wind through the side streets of the city. She stood up and told everyone that God was moving in the alleyways, not just the main streets, and that we were to pray that the hand of God would move people into the concealed places to keep divine appointments. That is exactly when you were moved to leave the main streets, go up that side street, and have that meeting with a seeker.'

We all praised God when we heard this!

Using Healing as Well as Prophecy

What did this incident teach us? Obviously it was a strong reminder of the priceless value of having prayer backing when teams go out on the streets to do any kind of evangelism. If it hadn't been for our intercessors back at the conference centre, I am not convinced that Graham and I would have kept this divine appointment.

At the same time, the whole episode was a very big lesson about the close relationship that exists between prophecy and healing in evangelism. When we go out into the work place or the community to evangelise, we should not expect just to operate in one gift. God wants to speak, yes, but he also wants to *act*! So it may well be the case that we hear him speaking about a person who doesn't know God. As we do so, we may be shown the secret things in that person's life. Those things could be sins, but they could just as likely be wounds hidden from everyone except God. When sins are exposed we should lead the person in the sinner's prayer so that they can receive forgiveness through the Cross. When wounds are exposed, we should pray for healing, with a view to sharing the Gospel as well.

So I see a very close relationship between prophecy and healing. Sometimes we hear what God is saying about a person's needs, and this leads us into experiencing the Lord's compassion for them. This in turn creates such an overwhelming desire to help that we virtually cannot resist the desire to offer to pray for them. Born of love and faith, the prayer ministry that follows is always powerful. Healing often follows hearing.

All this is perfectly biblical. The Lord Jesus only ever did what he saw the Father doing. How did he know what the Father was doing? Through the Holy Spirit operating in his life, giving Jesus a prophetic consciousness of the Father's voice. Through this gift Jesus knew the Father's will; he knew when to speak and when to act. This in turn led him into ministering to the sick and the oppressed. So, for Jesus too, hearing led to healing.

The first Christians also followed this pattern. The first major miracle described after the Pentecost event in Acts 2 is the healing of the lame man at the Gate Beautiful outside the Temple in Jerusalem. This is described in Acts 3. The story opens as follows, with Peter and John on their way to the Temple to keep one of the three daily Jewish times of prayer. As they do so they come into contact with a beggar who has been lame from birth. As a lame man, he is not allowed in the Temple, so he begs outside:

Peter and John went to the Temple one afternoon to take part in the three o'clock prayer service. As they approached the Temple, a man lame from birth was being carried in. Each day he was put beside the Temple gate, the one called the Beautiful Gate, so he could beg from the people going into the Temple.

When he saw Peter and John about to enter, he asked them for
some money (Acts 3:1–3).

Jesus had almost certainly walked past this man many
times. So had the apostles, including Peter and John. He
was obviously brought to this same spot three times
every day because it was a strategic place to beg. With
crowds of people going into the Temple to observe this
special hour of prayer, the opportunities for receiving
donations were excellent. However, on this day, the
beggar was destined to receive something far better than
money. He was going to get healed.

Let's see what happens. First of all, we read in verse 4,
'Peter and John looked at him intently.' Why did they
look at the man intently? The word in the original is
atenizo, which means 'to fasten one's eye on someone'.
Peter and John were looking intently at the man but they
were also listening attentively to the Father. My
conviction is that they were operating prophetically here,
trying to track what the Holy Spirit was doing in this
man's life. After a few moments they realised that it was
God's sovereign will right there and then to heal this
man. So we read:

Peter said, 'Look at us!' The lame man looked at them eagerly,
expecting a gift. But Peter said, 'I don't have any money for
you. But I'll give you what I have. In the name of Jesus Christ
of Nazareth, get up and walk!' Then Peter took the lame man
by the right hand and helped him up. And as he did, the man's
feet and anklebones were healed and strengthened. He jumped
up, stood on his feet, and began to walk! Then, walking,
leaping, and praising God, he went into the Temple with them.
All the people saw him walking and heard him praising God.
When they realised he was the lame beggar they had seen so

often at the Beautiful Gate, they were absolutely astounded!
They all rushed out to Solomon's Colonnade, where he was
holding tightly to Peter and John. Everyone stood there in awe
of the wonderful thing that had happened (Acts 3:4–11).

Having moved in the gift of prophecy, Peter and John
now pray for a miraculous healing. This duly happens
and all are amazed. Having been barred from the Temple
because of his lameness, the beggar now not only walks
into the Temple, he *leaps* there. All this in fulfilment of
what the prophet had said in Isaiah chapter 35:

Say to those who are afraid, 'Be strong, and do not fear, for
your God is coming to destroy your enemies. He is coming to
save you.' And when he comes, he will open the eyes of the blind
and unstop the ears of the deaf. The lame will leap like a deer,
and those who cannot speak will shout and sing (Is. 35:4–6)!

But the story doesn't end here. With the crowds now
marvelling at what has happened to this well-known
local beggar, Peter seizes the initiative and uses this
miracle as a platform for preaching the Gospel to
everyone within earshot. So we see in verse 12: 'Peter
saw his opportunity and addressed the crowd.'

What do we learn from this? That prophecy and healing
can work together very powerfully in our ministry to the
lost. The evidence both of what God reveals to an
unbeliever (through the prophetic) and of what God does
in that same person's life (through healing) can combine to
create levels of openness to the Gospel that a merely
intellectual approach could never achieve. I am not in any
way minimising the importance of being theologically
wise in what we say and do. Relying on gifts like prophecy
and healing is not a justification for lack of study,

preparation and understanding. But I have learned over the years that with evangelism there is no substitute for demonstrations of the Spirit's power.

An Old Testament Prototype

The combination of prophecy and healing in ministering to the lost is not unique to the New Testament. This combination of prophesying to and healing those outside God's people occurred before Jesus came. This is demonstrated in what is one of my favourite episodes in the Old Testament, the extraordinary transformation of a pagan man called Naaman. He went from being a worshipper of the Syrian god Rimmon to a worshipper of Yahweh in a matter of hours. The reason for this 'conversion' was his experience of healing at the hands of a prophet of Israel called Elisha. Indeed, in Elisha's ministry to this man we see a prototypical combination of prophecy and healing in evangelism.

The story is told in 2 Kings 5. It begins with a brief description of the general:

The king of Aram had high admiration for Naaman, the commander of his army, because through him the LORD had given Aram great victories. But though Naaman was a mighty warrior, he suffered from leprosy.

Naaman was a great military commander, highly esteemed by the Syrian king. He had everything going for him. He was successful in battle. The writer even says that his victories were God's doing. He really did have everything going for him except for one thing. As the Bible very briefly comments, 'he suffered from leprosy'.

However, this is not where the story ends. Naaman is about to have his whole life turned upside down. He is about to be introduced to a prophet of Israel called Elisha who will secure divine healing for him – a healing that will cause the general to come to know the one true God, the God of Israel, the God of Elisha.

But we are not quite there yet. How Naaman actually gets to meet Elisha is remarkable. The general only gets to hear about the possibility of his healing because of the testimony of a young girl – a girl whom his own troops had abducted from Israel's territory:

Now groups of Aramean raiders had invaded the land of Israel, and among their captives was a young girl who had been given to Naaman's wife as a maid. One day the girl said to her mistress, 'I wish my master would go to see the prophet in Samaria. He would heal him of his leprosy.' So Naaman told the king what the young girl from Israel had said. 'Go and visit the prophet,' the king told him. 'I will send a letter of introduction for you to carry to the king of Israel.' So Naaman started out, taking as gifts 750 pounds of silver, 150 pounds of gold, and ten sets of clothing. The letter to the king of Israel said: 'With this letter I present my servant Naaman. I want you to heal him of his leprosy' (2 Kgs. 5:2–6).

At this point the king of Israel enters the picture. In his paranoia he believes that Naaman's request is a trick. Elisha, however, hears about this and rescues the day:

When the king of Israel read it, he tore his clothes in dismay and said, 'This man sends me a leper to heal! Am I God, that I can kill and give life? He is only trying to find an excuse to invade us again.' But when Elisha, the man of God, heard about the king's reaction, he sent this message to him: 'Why

*are you so upset? Send Naaman to me, and he will learn that
there is a true prophet here in Israel.' (2 Kgs. 5:7–8)*

The key person in the story at this point is a child.
Naaman secured his reputation by organising military
raids into Syria. On one occasion he had captured and
adopted a very young Israelite girl. We do not know
exactly what happened, but she ended up as a maid to
Naaman's wife. When Naaman's leprosy began to be
both visible and known, this little girl did something
extraordinary. She told her mistress that she wished her
master, Naaman, would go to see the prophet in Israel
(Elisha). He would heal him, she adds.

Now these are the only words she speaks but they are
full of riches. First of all, they shine with *faith*. The little
girl (whose name is not recorded) was convinced that
Elisha would heal her master. There are no qualifying
statements. She just knows with childlike faith that her
master will receive healing, even though he is an enemy
of Israel. When I tell you that there was no evidence
behind her claim it is even more remarkable. Jesus was
later to say that Elisha only ever healed one person of
leprosy in his entire life, and that was a Syrian, i.e.
Naaman (Lk. 4: 27). There was no track record in Elisha's
ministry to give the young girl grounds for saying what
she did. Elisha had not healed any Israelite leper. But she
was walking by faith, not by sight. Indeed, she shows
far more faith and insight than the king of Israel.

The second thing that's remarkable about this little
girl's words is *forgiveness*. This child had every reason to
be bitter. She had been taken from her home. She had
been separated from her parents and her family (in all
likelihood killed). She had had her freedom removed
and she was living to all intents and purposes as a child

slave. But when she learns that the man responsible for all her suffering is himself suffering, she expresses her desire for him to be healed! This can only be because she had worked past her grief and anger to a place of acceptance and even forgiveness. If she had been bitter, she would never have said this and Naaman would never have heard about Elisha. In turn, this might have meant a gradual, humiliating and lonely death for Naaman. But she obviously forgave him. And in so doing she provided the bridge between her master and the prophet of Israel.

What a great testimony of the power of forgiveness! And what a great picture of the way God wants to use children in his Kingdom purposes!

So, Naaman reports to his king what the little girl has said and the king sends Naaman and a huge quantity of gifts to the king of Israel, who promptly suspects that this is a trick and that he is about to be conned into a major military disaster. Thankfully, Elisha hears what has happened and tells the king of Israel to send Naaman to him instead. So we read:

> *So Naaman went with his horses and chariots and waited at the door of Elisha's house. But Elisha sent a messenger out to him with this message: 'Go and wash yourself seven times in the River Jordan. Then your skin will be restored, and you will be healed of leprosy' (2 Kgs. 5:9–10).*

Notice how Elisha does not come out in person, even though Naaman is a VIP. Elisha is exercising great wisdom here. He doesn't want Naaman to think that he is responsible for what is about to happen. He wants Naaman to know that it is God. Naaman, however, does not understand this yet and becomes indignant:

But Naaman became angry and stalked away. 'I thought he would surely come out to meet me!' he said. 'I expected him to wave his hand over the leprosy and call on the name of the LORD his God and heal me! Aren't the River Abana and River Pharpar of Damascus better than all the rivers of Israel put together? Why shouldn't I wash in them and be healed?' So Naaman turned and went away in a rage. But his officers tried to reason with him and said, 'Sir, if the prophet had told you to do some great thing, wouldn't you have done it? So you should certainly obey him when he says simply to go and wash and be cured!' So Naaman went down to the River Jordan and dipped himself seven times, as the man of God had instructed him. And his flesh became as healthy as a young child's, and he was healed! (2 Kgs. 5:11–14).

Thankfully Naaman had the humility to listen to his servants and he was healed in the River Jordan.

Then Naaman and his entire party went back to find the man of God. They stood before him, and Naaman said, 'I know at last that there is no God in all the world except in Israel. Now please accept my gifts.' But Elisha replied, 'As surely as the LORD lives, whom I serve, I will not accept any gifts.' And though Naaman urged him to take the gifts, Elisha refused. Then Naaman said, 'All right, but please allow me to load two of my mules with earth from this place, and I will take it back home with me. From now on I will never again offer any burnt offerings or sacrifices to any other god except the LORD. However, may the LORD pardon me in this one thing. When my master the king goes into the temple of the god Rimmon to worship there and leans on my arm, may the LORD pardon me when I bow, too.' 'Go in peace,' Elisha said. So Naaman started home again (2 Kgs. 5:15–19).

There is so much one could say about these verses. But the main thing I want to stress is the way in which Elisha operates not only prophetically but also in faith for healing. He knows what God wants for this general, even though he is a pagan and an enemy of Israel. With a mind unclouded by prejudice, Elisha sees what God is doing and sends the general to wash in the River Jordan where he is completely healed. This leads Naaman to acknowledge that there is only one God, the God of Israel. It also leads him to want to give up worshipping the pagan god of his own nation.

Three characters are worthy of attention in this story: the general, the child and the prophet. The general is emphatically lost. He is a sinner and he is also sick. But the Lord uses a little girl to bring him into contact with an Old Testament version of a prophetic evangelist – a man called Elisha who not only ministers in prophecy but also in healing. Using both these gifts in a very wise and compassionate way, Elisha causes the pagan general to come to confess Israel's God as the one true God. Here once again we see how potent the gifts of prophecy and healing can be in leading lost people to believe in the one true God.

Hearing and Healing

This story is really important because Elisha has always been seen as a type, or a foreshadowing, of Jesus Christ. Elijah brought a message of God's judgement whereas Elisha brought a message of salvation. This corresponds with John the Baptist and Jesus. John was the one like Elijah who called the people to repentance. Jesus was one like Elisha who brought the Good News of God's mercy and forgiveness for everyone. Indeed, like Elisha, Jesus ministered effectively to the condition of leprosy.

Jesus only said what he heard the Father saying. In other

words, he listened to the prophetic voice of God. Jesus only ever did what he saw the Father doing. This involved healing the sick. This combination of hearing and healing is really important today, and it is important not just in the church among believers but outside the church among the lost. There is no doubt that praying for unbelievers to receive healing in Jesus' name has extraordinary effects. At the very least they experience the power of God in their lives (which is a testimony in itself). When we receive a prophetic word for an unbeliever the effect is even more powerful. While healing prayer makes people generally aware that God is alive and that he loves them, a specific prophetic word makes them especially aware of this fact. The healing presence of God is wonderful. A very personal word from God is even more wonderful. It shows that God knows the person by name. It also evokes faith in their hearts because faith comes by *hearing*.

All this suggests the vital importance of being sensitive to the healing presence of God when ministering in prophetic evangelism. God will spotlight people and give us revelation about them, if we ask him to. When we start ministering in this way we will find ourselves drawn to unbelievers who need healing. When that happens God wants us to be bold and ask whether that person would like prayer. The power of God's word and God's works will cause that unbeliever to move quickly from hostility to receptivity as regards the Gospel.

Praying for Seekers

When it comes to ministering healing to those who are not Christians, there are a few practical things I would like to share.

First, it is really important to be clear about the person's name and their need. You want to mention their name before the Father and you want to be open about their condition. A few minutes in conversation will be enough to get all the vital information.

Second, it is vital to share a very brief testimony with them. Say something like this: 'I am a Christian and I really believe that Jesus saves, Jesus heals, Jesus delivers. We have seen people healed through prayer in Jesus' name.'

Third, always ask the person for permission to pray. Say something like, 'Would you like me to pray for you?'

Fourth, if they say yes, tell them what is involved. Say that it won't take long and that you are going to invite the Holy Spirit to come and minister healing to the condition in Jesus' name. Ask them to extend their arms and hold their hands out to receive.

Fifth, *pray*! There is one golden rule here, though: be brief. Jesus did not pray at great length when he ministered healing to those who were not his followers. He prayed simply and with authority. We need to do the same. Religious and lengthy prayers are not necessary and indeed frequently off-putting. Pray succinctly and with faith.

Sixth, track what the Holy Spirit is saying and doing. It is so fascinating the way those who have never heard about what happens when people receive prayer experience the very phenomena we see in church. They experience sensations of warmth, heat, tingling, and so on. Their hands may shake and their eyelids flutter. This is the moment to share prophetic words the Lord gives you. Let them bask in the embrace of the Father's love for a few moments after praying.

Seventh, ask them how they feel and what they sensed was going on. Encourage them to believe that God was doing something in their lives. Don't make promises but do point to the things that indicate that God has touched them.

Finally, always point away from yourself when they ask, 'What was that?' Unbelievers will never have experienced anything like this before. It is important that you tell them that it isn't you, it isn't some nebulous force, but the Lord Jesus, who loves them personally. Ask them if they'd like to know more. Direct them to a church where they will receive more of what they have just heard about and experienced. Encourage them to go on an Alpha Course. Do what Peter did in Acts 3: seize the day!

> *Peter saw his opportunity and addressed the crowd. 'People of Israel,' he said, 'what is so astounding about this? And why look at us as though we had made this man walk by our own power and godliness? For it is the God of Abraham, the God of Isaac, the God of Jacob, the God of all our ancestors who has brought glory to his servant Jesus by doing this. This is the same Jesus whom you handed over and rejected before Pilate, despite Pilate's decision to release him. You rejected this holy, righteous one and instead demanded the release of a murderer. You killed the author of life, but God raised him to life. And we are witnesses of this fact!' (Acts 3:12–15).*

Chapter 9

REASONS FOR GETTING STARTED

Someone sent me this interesting contrast between the reproductive habits of elephants and rabbits:

Elephants:
- Only fertile four times a year
- Only one baby per pregnancy
- 22-month gestation period
- Sexual maturity: eighteen years
- Maximum growth potential in three years: one elephant

Rabbits:
- Almost continuously fertile
- Average of seven babies per pregnancy
- One-month gestation period
- Sexual maturity: four months
- Maximum growth potential in three years: 476 million rabbits

Most of us, when it comes to evangelism, are much more like elephants than rabbits! We know that Jesus has called us to bear much fruit and to reproduce in others the life that he has invested in us. We know we are called to sow the seed of God's word in other people's lives and to see multiplied growth – thirty, sixty, one hundred times. However, if we're really honest, we also know that we are much more like elephants than rabbits. We think about evangelism about four times a year and we might lead a person to Christ every three years at best.

One of the joys of using prophecy in evangelism is that it is a fruitful method. The gift of prophecy leads to far greater effectiveness in witnessing to our family, friends, neighbours, work colleagues and those we bump into. For this reason alone I believe it is a method worth developing both individually and corporately in the church. In case you still need persuading, let me offer my top ten reasons for getting started on the road of prophetic evangelism.

1. Because it is a Biblical Method

We have seen throughout this book that prophetic evangelism is very much God's idea, not ours. It is not a humanly devised methodology. Throughout the Bible we find God's people using prophecy not only in their ministry to one another but also to those who don't know God. In the Old Testament we mentioned Joseph, Elijah, Elisha and Daniel. The witness of the New Testament is even more striking. Jesus used prophecy in his ministry to lost people. So did Peter (Acts 3 and 10), Philip (Acts 8:26–40) and Paul (Acts 16:8–10). In fact Paul was actually converted as a result of a vision of the ascended Lord Jesus and hearing his voice (Acts 9:2–6). He is led into the Kingdom of God by a man who is given Paul's address and destiny in a vision (Ananias, Acts 9:10–12). Here again we see both Type A and Type B prophetic evangelism.

In the light of all this evidence it is abundantly clear that God's people have consistently used prophecy in evangelism. Nothing in the pages of the New Testament suggests that prophecy is only to be used within the church among believers. We have already seen how the view that prophecy is a believers-only phenomenon is based on a wrong interpretation of 1 Corinthians 14:20–25. The Bible as a whole bears testimony to the fact that prophecy is supposed to benefit unbelievers, not just believers.

Furthermore, there is nothing in the pages of the New Testament to suggest that prophecy was only supposed to be used in the first century. Rather, we are taught that we will go on prophesying until Jesus comes back. As Paul wrote in 1 Corinthians 13:9–10, 'Now we know only a little, and even the gift of prophecy reveals little! But when the end comes, these special gifts will all disappear.'

When Jesus comes back at the end of history, prophecy will become redundant. Until then, God's people have been empowered to witness prophetically.

2. Because it is What Jesus Did

Jesus consistently operated in the gift of prophecy in his ministry to the lost. In fact, one of the distinctive features of Jesus' life is what theologians call *cardiagnosis*. This is a Greek word combining *gnosis*, meaning 'knowledge', with *cardia*, meaning 'heart'. Jesus had a special knowledge of the human heart. By prophetic revelation he read the lives of everyone he met.

So, in Mark 2:1–12, while Jesus is teaching in Simon Peter's house in Capernaum, a stretcher is lowered through the roof. On the stretcher is a paralysed man. Jesus, by prophetic revelation, sees that the man's friends have faith and that the sick man needs to receive forgiveness for his sins before he can receive physical healing. In addition, Mark tells us that Jesus knew full well in his spirit what the scribes were saying to themselves (literally, within their hearts).

In Luke 5:1–11, when Jesus meets Peter at the lake, he sees where the fish are and tells Peter (who has been out fishing all night and caught nothing) to push out into deep water and put down his nets. Peter does so and catches a great number of fish. Peter now realises that he has someone on board his boat who can see everything, including his own heart. So he tells Jesus to leave because he, Peter, is a man of sin. Jesus, however, prophesies over Peter and his colleagues that they will become fishers of men.

The same is true in the story of Zacchaeus in Luke 19:1–10. Jesus sees Zacchaeus hiding in a tree, knows his name by divine revelation, and calls out to Zacchaeus that he wants to have a meal with him. Again, this is Jesus using prophecy in evangelism.

In John's gospel this is a common theme. Jesus wins both Nathanael (Jn. 1:43–51) and the Samaritan woman (Jn. 4:4–42) using prophecy. The gospel writer tells us that Jesus knew what was in other people's hearts (Jn. 2:25, NIV). The conclusion is inescapable: Jesus listened prophetically to what the Father was saying in his ministry to the lost. This is one of the major characteristics of his earthly ministry.

3. Because it is Something We can Do

Sometimes people say that Jesus had these insights because he was the Son of God. Behind this statement lies the view that Jesus' insights into other people's hearts were somehow the product of his divinity. They argue that we are not, of course, like Jesus in this sense. We are therefore not to expect to have this level of revelation about others.

While I understand why people express this view, I do not accept it as valid. Jesus possessed charismatic insight and foresight as a result of the gift of prophecy. The evidence for this is the fact that his own contemporaries regarded his special insights not as evidence that he was divine but as evidence that he was a prophet. Thus, when Jesus saw the secret history of the Samaritan woman, she said, 'Sir, you must be a prophet,' not, 'Sir, you must be God.' (Jn. 4:19)

In Luke 7:36–39 a Pharisee invites Jesus to dinner. An immoral woman hears that Jesus is in the house and enters uninvited to pour expensive perfume over his feet. She keeps weeping over his feet and kissing them as she applies the perfume. What Luke says next is revealing:

When the Pharisee who was the host saw what was happening and who the woman was, he said to himself, 'This proves that Jesus is no prophet. If God had really sent him, he would know what kind of woman is touching him. She's a sinner!' (Lk. 7:39).

The Pharisee's reasoning is valid but his conclusions are wrong. Seeing into the heart of another is indeed a hallmark of the prophetic. Jesus *does* see what the woman is like, but the wonder of the scene is that he lets her minister to him anyway.

The historical Jesus was God in human flesh, yes, but his insights and foresight were due to the gift of prophecy at work in his life. This should fill us with hope. This means that we too can use prophecy in our ministry to the lost. Just as Jesus in his humanity depended on the revelatory gifts, so can we.

4. Because it Exposes Secret Sins

When believers operate in the gift of prophecy, secret hang-ups, habits and hurts are exposed. This happens in the church first of all. The story of Ananias and Sapphira is a telling reminder. They tried to keep secret that they were withholding some of their financial giving. In Acts 5, Peter sees prophetically what Ananias has been up to and challenges him:

> *'Ananias, why has Satan filled your heart? You lied to the Holy Spirit, and you kept some of the money for yourself. The property was yours to sell or not sell, as you wished. And after selling it, the money was yours to give away. How could you do a thing like this? You weren't lying to us but to God' (Acts 5:3–4).*

At this, Ananias drops dead. Three hours later the same thing happens to his wife Sapphira. Luke concludes by saying, 'Great fear gripped the entire church and all others who heard what had happened.'

There is no doubt about it: using prophecy among believers produces higher levels of holiness and wholeness. People realise that it is far harder to hide their sins and wounds when those around them can see into their hearts. I like what Professor James Dunn says about these effects of genuine prophecy:

> Prophecy prevents a man pretending to be other than he is – prevents the believer hiding behind a mask of pretended righteousness, of apparent spirituality. At any time the prophetic word may expose him for what he is. He dare not take refuge in the image he portrays to the world, in his reputation, in arguments, in self-justification. Where the prophetic Spirit is present, honesty with oneself and about oneself is indispensable.

Prophecy can have the same effect on unbelievers, as Paul testifies in 1 Corinthians 14:20–25. Prophecy brings unbelievers to a true realisation of their sinfulness.

In this respect we should remember that God has already made very plain in his Word what he regards as sinful and unholy. The Ten Commandments, in particular, show us what he regards as unlawful. For many centuries these formed the foundation not only for morality but also for the legal system in the UK. As someone once said, 'Men and women are able creatures; we have made over 32 million laws and haven't yet improved on the Ten Commandments.' Elton Trueblood's summary of these Commandments goes like this:

> Above all else love God alone;
> Bow down to neither wood nor stone.
> God's name refuse to take in vain;
> The Sabbath rest with care maintain.
> Respect your parents all your days;
> Hold sacred human life always.
> Be loyal to your chosen mate;
> Steal nothing, neither small nor great.
> Report, with truth, your neighbour's deed;
> And rid your mind of selfish greed.

Prophetic words for unbelievers very often expose where they have broken one or more of these commandments. Sharon Stone writes:

> One afternoon, two young ladies from my office went to a nearby shop to buy some lunch. While they were there, two men tried to 'pick them up'. The girls, being a little naïve, didn't realise what the men were trying to do.

Seeing that the men were so friendly they thought this was a good opportunity to operate in prophetic evangelism. One of the ladies received a word from the Lord for one of the men. She was so excited that God had given her something that she could not wait to say it. She turned to him and said, 'God just told me that he can forgive anything, including murder.' As it turned out, the man had committed murder and it was the key that unlocked his heart to receiving Jesus into his life.

Truly, prophetic evangelism exposes secret sins.

5. Because it Lets God Take the Lead

Someone has defined mission as finding out what God is doing and then joining in. This is a perfect summary of why prophetic evangelism is such a great resource. With this method, God is the one who takes the initiative. We cooperate with what the Holy Spirit is saying and doing as he connects us with people who are ready to hear the Good News about Jesus.

When I conduct weekends on prophetic evangelism, we move from teaching in the church or conference centre onto the streets to 'do the stuff', as John Wimber used to call it. One of the things I stress before people leave is the fact that their role is to see what the Father is doing. He is sovereign in the process. The disadvantage of this kind of thinking, of course, is that it can make people passive in evangelism. This needs to be discouraged. The advantage is that many people find this liberating. It causes them to let God be God, with the additional benefit that they become more open to 'having a go'.

The truth is many have been put off evangelism because

it has been rammed into them that they have to do all the running, they have to witness to a certain number of people, in short they have to do it all. This puts intolerable strain on people and creates a guilt-edged religion. With prophetic evangelism we recognise that if nothing happens it may be because God did not give us a green light. Of course it may also be that we simply didn't obey what the Lord told us! Nevertheless, the truth is we cannot orchestrate divine appointments. Prophetic revelation isn't available on tap, either. Our part is to be available, to be alert, and to be active when the Father wants to use us. Our task is to look out for the son or daughter of peace (the one in whom God is already working). As Jesus says in Luke 10:5–6, 'Whatever house you enter, first say, "Peace be to this house!" And if a son of peace is there, your peace shall rest upon him; but if not, it shall return to you' (RSV).

6. Because it is a Two-Edged Sword

A prophetic word proves that God is real and that he knows every detail of a person's life. Prophetic revelation is a lethal weapon in spiritual warfare. It penetrates the defences people put up against God.

The writer to the Hebrews says this about the living word of God. In this instance, 'the word of God' is simply what God says. It can refer to any example of God speaking. Primarily this means Scripture, but it could also refer to prophetic words:

For the word of God is living and active. Sharper than any double-edged sword, it penetrates even to dividing soul and spirit, joints and marrow; it judges the thoughts and attitudes of the heart. Nothing in all creation is hidden from God's sight. Everything is uncovered and laid bare before the eyes of him to whom we must give account (Heb. 4:12–13, NIV).

These verses speak of the living word of God penetrating between the soul and the spirit. While some commentators insist that we should not make too much of the difference between soul (*psyche*) and spirit (*pneuma*), I beg to disagree. I do not personally believe that the Bible gives us a bipartite view of human beings – a view that says we are made of two parts, body and soul. That is more a product of Greek dualism than of the Hebrew Scriptures. Rather, I believe that verses like 1 Thessalonians 5:23 portray us as being tripartite – as made up of three parts, the body (*soma*), the soul (*psyche*) and the spirit (*pneuma*).

What is the difference between these three? The body is the physical part of our being, that relates to the material world around us. The soul is made up of our minds, emotions and will. The spirit is that part of us created to commune with God. Until we are born again, the spirit is dead and the soul is hostile and rebellious towards God. When we receive pardon at the Cross of Christ, our spirits are made alive and our souls become docile and receptive towards God.

Some argue that the 'living word of God' can only mean the Scriptures. While this is possible, I agree with Donald Hagner, who says this about Hebrews 4:12:

The **word of God** is neither a reference to Jesus nor even primarily to Scripture. It is instead what God speaks, and the idea was probably suggested to the author from the repeated reference to 'hearing God's voice' in the preceding verses (3:7, 15–16; 4:2, 7). God's voice, the **word of God**, by its very character demands authentic response.

I think Hagner is right that the living word of God is what

God speaks. The living word of God is received wherever and whenever God's voice is heard. This will most often be through the Bible, but it could be through prophecy.

All this is relevant to the subject of prophetic evangelism. A living, active word from God can penetrate through the hostile mind, the hard heart and the stubborn will (the soul) and pierce the spirit of an unbeliever. A prophetic word given to an unbeliever pierces their defences and creates a spark of light and life in their spirit. For a moment there is a spark of illumination. God is revealed as both alive and personal. Prophecy is accordingly vital for effective evangelism.

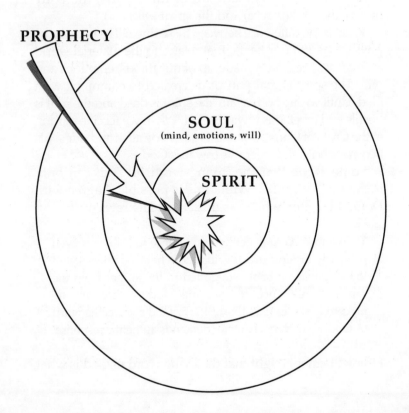

PROPHECY

SOUL
(mind, emotions, will)

SPIRIT

7. Because it Softens People's Hearts

Prophecy greatly increases an unbeliever's openness to the Gospel. It can turn an unbeliever from hostility to receptivity in a very short time.

We need to remind ourselves that evangelism is a process, and that sometimes this process can take a very long time. It can take years for some people to make the journey from unbelief to saving faith:

| -10 | -9 | -8 | -7 | -6 | -5 | -4 | -3 | -2 | -1 | 0 | +1 |

Unbelief   **Faith**

Using prophecy in evangelism accelerates the process. It creates an openness to the Gospel in a way that mere reasoning could never do.

My friend, Bruce Collins, has written a book simply entitled *Prophesy*. It is the only book about prophecy that has a chapter on using prophecy in evangelism. In it Bruce tells the story of how he was on a flight to Finland. A smartly dressed lady in her forties came and sat in the seat next to him. He prayed for revelation about her and, at an opportune moment, spoke it out. Bruce shared prophetic insights about her being a teacher with a real care for the poor and the oppressed. She was absolutely stunned. It turned out that she was a lecturer in international law and that her subject was law relating to international human rights (particularly those of oppressed peoples). Bruce says that her newspaper stayed on the floor for the rest of the flight as she asked questions about Christianity. As they left the aircraft, Bruce found out where she lived and told her where the nearest Alpha Course to her home was.

Bruce says that a prophetic word can turn an atheist into a seeker in thirty seconds. That's what happened in the incident on the plane. That is what happened to the woman of Samaria (Jn. 4:4–42). That's what can happen to those we meet, if we keep in step with the Spirit. A prophetic word can soften the hearts of unbelievers.

8. Because it is What God's Saying

As I have stepped out in faith, teaching about prophetic evangelism and attempting to practise it, I have come across prophetic people who have been saying for a while that this is something that God was going to birth in his church.

Larry Randolph wrote in 1995 that most believers were not using prophecy in evangelism at that time. In his book, *User Friendly Prophecy*, he identifies three reasons why this might have been the case. First, many evangelical churches don't believe in the gift of prophecy. Second, those who do believe never take it outside the walls of their own churches. Third, people want to use prophecy in public (where they can get kudos), not in private (where there is no honour). However, Larry Randolph made this comment on p.90:

> I believe that this is going to change in the near future. My hope is that thousands of prophetic people will flood the market place and job sites, bringing conviction through the gift of prophecy. I can almost envision a sign on the church door that states, 'Sorry, this institution is closed today; we've gone fishing for people.'

Larry Randolph is not alone in prophesying this. John Paul Jackson has written in an e-mail article that 'in the coming days, prophetic evangelism is about to flourish as never before'.

While it has always been possible for God's people to use prophecy in witnessing to the lost, it seems that right now God is stressing this method in a major way. As I wrote in chapter 2, it is not the only way of evangelising. But it is seemingly a way that the Holy Spirit is calling us to walk right now. People that I regard as prophetic are emphasizing this. As John said, 'Anyone who is willing to hear should listen to the Spirit and understand what the Spirit is saying to the churches' (Rev. 2:7).

9. Because it is Effective Today

Dana Scully, in an episode of *The X Files* called 'Revelations', is asked this question: 'What are you afraid of? That God isn't speaking?' She replies, 'No: that he is speaking, but no one is listening.'

In our culture, prophecy is effective because unbelievers are very open to receiving supernatural revelation. Of course, just because something seems to work well in our culture does not mean that it is necessarily right. Nevertheless, we have seen in this book that God's people are called to desire prophecy and to use this gift in witnessing. More than that, people in both the Old and the New Testament model and teach prophetic evangelism. This includes Jesus himself. In other words, we have seen that there is an objective reason for using prophetic evangelism that goes beyond mere 'pragmatism'. It is not just the case that it's workable. It's the case that it's biblical!

One of the reasons why prophetic evangelism is so

important is because Western society is now very open to the mystical and the numinous. This is mainly because we have moved from modernity to postmodernity. The modernist mindset put reason as the primary arbiter of what is true. The postmodernist mindset gives primary place to experience, even spiritual experience.

A friend of mine was sitting next to a woman on an underground train. Suddenly she felt God speaking to her about the person. She turned to her and just simply said, 'You're looking for God, aren't you?'

The woman's eyes started to fill with tears and she said, 'How did you know?' My friend replied, 'Because God just told me. And he also told me that you're looking for him in the wrong place.'

My friend then shared her testimony and directed the woman to the Alpha Course nearest to where she lived.

It is *not* the case any longer that people aren't looking for God. Postmodern people are looking but they are looking in the wrong places. Prophecy is a great resource for getting people's attention. It is a particularly effective tool in postmodernity.

Doug Addison gives a graphic example of the effectiveness of prophetic evangelism in contemporary culture. He writes:

As I was sitting comfortably in front of a Starbucks recently, I looked down and saw a yellow spider crawling on my knee. Immediately I heard the Holy Spirit say, 'You are about to have an encounter with someone in the New Age.' Symbolically, spiders often represent occult spirits. About 30 minutes later I was knee-deep in a God-orchestrated encounter with a woman and her friend. She seemed very open as I told her the meaning of the dream she had shared with me. I noticed that she did not have any walls or barriers up so I took the conversation to the next level. I asked the Holy Spirit about her and her friend and I repeated to her what I had heard. 'You do something eith your hands and it brings healing to people.' It turned out she was a New Age massage therapist.

I then looked to her friend and told her what I had heard as well. 'There is something important about the color pink.' They both burst into laughter because she had just painted her bedroom pink and she hated pink. Going back to the first woman, I heard the Holy Spirit say, 'Ask her about her spirit guides.' She leaned in and said in a low voice, 'I am so glad you asked. I think one of them might be bad for me.'

The encounter went on for several minutes and by this time any walls they had had up were somewhere in China. I told them I was a Christian and not a psychic, but I was not like any Christian they had ever met. 'I'll say! they replied. I went on to tell them about new light that was coming into their lives. One of them said, 'I have been asking for new light.'

I briefly told the first woman that her traditional religious upbringing would soon make more sense. It was then that I sensed a hesitation in her. I took it as far as I could without damaging what God had already done. Both she and her friend were amazed that a Christian could tell them about their lives so accurately. It was now up to the Holy Spirit to send someone to follow up and bring them closer to him. I got their first names and have been praying for them on a regular basis.

We are regularly seeing encounters like the one I described and these encounters seem to be increasing as we go places and make ourselves available to God.

10. Because it is Part of God's Plan

On the Day of Pentecost, 120 believers were filled with
the Holy Spirit and started declaring the wonders of God
in unlearned foreign languages. The Apostle Peter stood
up and declared that what was happening was in
fulfilment of Joel 2. The first part of the quotation talks
about the creation of a prophetic people:

*In the last days, God said, I will pour out my Spirit upon all
people. Your sons and daughters will prophesy, your young
men will see visions, and your old men will dream dreams. In
those days I will pour out my Spirit upon all my servants,
men and women alike, and they will prophesy (Acts 2:17–18).*

The last part of the quotation talks about the lost:

*And anyone who calls on the name of the Lord will be saved
(Acts 2:21).*

It has always been God's divine intent to create a church
that functioned as a 'prophetic family'. God's people are
to be prophetic. This applies to believers of all ages and
of every background. No believer is to be exempt. Every
one of us is supposed to have the gift of prophecy.

God established this prophetic family on the Day of
Pentecost two thousand years ago. On that day, 'the last
days of history' were inaugurated. The nearer we get to
Christ's return, the more we will see the church operating
in high-level prophecy. As that happens, we will see more
and more lost people calling on the name of the Lord to
be saved.

As an increasingly prophetic church connects with an
increasingly desperate world, I believe there will be

spiritual harvests as on the Day of Pentecost, when three thousand people were saved at the end of one sermon.

It is God's plan for us to use prophecy in evangelism.

Increasing in Fruitfulness

So here are ten reasons to motivate us to get started in prophetic evangelism:

- Because it is a biblical method
- Because it is what Jesus did
- Because it is something we can do
- Because it exposes secret sins
- Because it lets God take the lead
- Because it is a two-edged sword
- Because it softens people's hearts
- Because it is what God's saying
- Because it is effective today
- Because it is part of God's plan

I began this chapter by suggesting that many of us are more like elephants than rabbits when it comes to evangelising unbelievers. We want to be more fruitful but the truth is we are not really alert to the opportunities and we are not very effective when we do share. Perhaps, in the final analysis, this is because we are relying too much on our own strength and ideas rather than on the Holy Spirit. In prophetic evangelism, the Holy Spirit spotlights someone he wants to speak to, and the Holy Spirit gives us the revelation that leads a person to Christ. Using prophecy in evangelism is therefore a key to greater fruitfulness in our outreach to others. It is not a magic wand, nor is it the latest charismatic 'fad'. It is a biblical method that is extremely effective.

Throughout this book I have found Paul's words in 1 Corinthians 14:24–25 absolutely inspirational. There he writes:

> *If all of you are prophesying, and unbelievers or people who don't understand these things come into your meeting, they will be convicted of sin, and they will be condemned by what you say. As they listen, their secret thoughts will be laid bare, and they will fall down on their knees and worship God, declaring, 'God is really here among you.'*

The commentators suggest a number of possible Old Testament verses that may have influenced the words, 'God is really here among you.' One of them is Zechariah 8:23. This verse is the last of ten great promises for the Jewish people contained in that chapter. The church has been grafted onto the olive tree of biblical Judaism (Rom. 11). Even though this promise ultimately refers to the time when all Israel is saved (Rom. 11:26), there are good grounds for applying it to the church in this generation as well. Here is what the prophet says:

> *This is what the LORD Almighty says: In those days ten people from nations and languages around the world will clutch at the hem of one Jew's robe. And they will say, 'Please let us walk with you, for we have heard that God is with you' (Zech. 8:23).*

I long for the day when believers are so obviously bearing God's presence that unbelievers are magnetically drawn to us. Prophecy, according to Paul, is a manifestation of God's presence. It is a sign to believers that God is pleased and God is present. At the same time, it shows unbelievers that God is not above us or against us but rather among us. This makes believers contagious. In fact, Zechariah promises that ten unbelievers will grab hold of one believer because of this sense of the Lord's prophetic presence.

Though I do not necessarily equate fruitfulness with numbers, I like very much the idea of every believer having an impact on ten unbelievers. If an increase in prophecy will make us this fruitful in witnessing, then that is a great reason for getting started with prophetic evangelism. The ten reasons given in the course of this chapter will also, I pray, motivate you to believe that God can use you in this way too.

Chapter 10

BECOMING A PROPHETIC
EVANGELIST

When I was conducting a training conference abroad, I was asked whether I thought prophetic evangelism was something every believer can do. This is a really good question and required some thought.

My view is that we are all called to desire the spiritual gifts, and especially the gift of prophecy (1 Cor. 14:1). The outpouring of the Day of Pentecost has resulted in all of God's people being able now to prophesy, not just an elite few. I appreciate that some are called to have a ministry of prophecy (Eph. 4:11). At the same time, while not all of us may have the 'ministry' of prophecy, all of us can have the 'gift'.

Furthermore, all of us are called to witness to others about Jesus. This is not the same as being an evangelist. Evangelists are especially anointed to communicate the Gospel. These specialists are like barristers in a court of law. The rest of us are like the witnesses who are called to give evidence. Now that's something all of us can do and all of us are called to do. When Jesus made the promise in Acts 1:8 he was talking not just to the apostles but to the whole assembled church of 120:

But you will receive power when the Holy Spirit comes on you; and you will be my witnesses in Jerusalem, and in all Judea and Samaria, and to the ends of the earth (NIV).

172

I believe that all of us are to desire the gift of prophecy and all of us are called to witness. Put the two together and you reach the conclusion that every believer at least has the potential to witness prophetically and even to grow into a prophetic evangelist.

Having said that, I recognise that there are some people for whom prophecy and evangelism are their base or regular ministries, while for others they are more like a phase or an irregular ministry. For the former, prophetic evangelism will be a way of life. For the latter, it will be more occasional but no less powerful. Either way, we can all do it!

To put it succinctly, all believers can *potentially* engage in prophetic evangelism. However, only some believers engage in this ministry in *actual* practice.

What most believers need to do is to start! No one becomes a prophetic evangelist instantly. It takes time to grow into someone who is both confident and proficient in this ministry. No one is born into the world fully-grown and mature. We are born as babies, and babies cannot walk before they have learned how to crawl. So it is in the spiritual. When it comes to learning the art of prophetic evangelism we have to engage in a process of gradual development. This can involve growing pains. In fact, it is unlikely that anyone is going to develop into an effective prophetic evangelist without suffering. As Paul says in 2 Corinthians 1: 5–7:

> *You can be sure that the more we suffer for Christ, the more God will shower us with his comfort through Christ. So when we are weighed down with troubles, it is for your benefit and salvation! For when God comforts us, it is so that we, in turn, can be an encouragement to you. Then you can patiently endure the same things we suffer. We are confident that as you share in suffering, you will also share God's comfort.*

There are no shortcuts to growing into a prophetic evangelist. Look at Simon Peter. Jesus called him to be a fisher of men. Peter then spent three years in training. He then suffered the humiliation of denying Jesus before being reinstated and filled with the Holy Spirit. Only then did he start functioning effectively as a prophetic evangelist. In fact, it is not until we get to Acts 10 (well after Pentecost) that we see him really flowing in this ministry. Even then he initially says 'no' to God's voice when he hears it in an open vision. The development of Peter took time.

What can we do to grow into a ministry of prophetic evangelism, even if this is our phase rather than base ministry? In the following pages I will suggest a number of practical measures we might take.

First, Make Evangelism a Personal Priority

We will never get very far until we have first renounced our reluctance to engage in witnessing to unbelievers. This reluctance is widespread in the church today. We need to remember that there is an inextricable bond connecting following and fishing. Remember Luke 5:10–11?

Jesus replied to Simon, 'Don't be afraid! From now on you'll be fishing for people!' And as soon as they landed, they left everything and followed Jesus.

For Simon Peter, following Jesus meant fishing for men and women. Being a disciple meant evangelism!

Sooner or later we are going to have to get over our problem with what is today called the 'e'-word – the word 'evangelism'. In many churches this has become a taboo. What really matters is feeding those who are already members, not attracting those who are not. This has created a situation where the only increase in numbers usually comes through transfer growth rather than through evangelism. In other words, many churches grow not because they are winning the lost but because Christians from other churches are joining them.

The late Sam Shoemaker, an Episcopalian bishop, summed up the situation this way: 'In the Great Commission the Lord has called us to be – like Peter – fishers of men. We've turned the commission around so that we have become merely keepers of the aquarium. Occasionally I take some fish out of your fishbowl and put them into mine, and you do the same with my bowl. But we're all tending the same fish.'

If we are to engage in prophetic evangelism we must make evangelism a personal priority in our lives. The church that I lead is called St Andrew's. I pointed out several years ago that Andrew was the first evangelist in the Gospels. He found his brother Simon Peter. He told him about Jesus. And he brought him to Jesus. Finding, telling, bringing – that's what Andrew was into.

*Andrew, Simon Peter's brother, was one of these men who had heard what John said and then followed Jesus. The first thing Andrew did was to **find** his brother, Simon, and **tell** him, 'We have found the Messiah' (which means the Christ). Then Andrew **brought** Simon to meet Jesus (Jn. 1:40–42).*

This is what I have called our church to get back to, the ministry of the first evangelist, Andrew. John tells us that this was 'the *first* thing Andrew did'. It was a personal priority of Andrew's to evangelise.

My friend Phil Baker is a senior pastor in Perth, Australia. He and I share a great love of cricket and last

year I had the privilege of ministering in his church
while England were playing their test match in that city.
It was a great time of friendship and fun!

But it was also a great time of learning and input. Phil
has seen his church grow to three thousand through
evangelism. In fact, Riverview Church, Perth, is now the
largest church in western Australia.

One of the things I've learnt from Phil is the importance
of urging every member to become intentional about
inviting unbelievers to hear about Jesus. Phil talks about the
front door and back door of every church. The front door is
made up of EP and IR. EP means evangelistic potential –
how potent the church is for outsiders. IR is invitational ratio
– the number of members who are actually inviting non-
Christians to services. The back door is made up of RR and
AR. RR is the retention rate, the number of people who stay
and become committed members. AR is the attrition rate,
the number of people who leave because of moving house,
death, or other reasons.

Phil taught me one big lesson. He said that you can
have the most evangelistically potent church in the
world, but if the members are not into inviting their
friends, it's pointless. IR is the key. Individual members
need to make evangelism a personal priority. This for me
is the real key to church growth, and it is the key to
prophetic witnessing. We must prioritise evangelism.

Second, Ask God for More of the Prophetic

Several years ago I realised that there was so much more
I could experience in the area of prophecy. I was
receiving occasional dreams, visions and impressions,
but I knew there was a greater level of authority and

accuracy out there. So I started praying every day on the basis of the promise of Jesus in Matthew 7:11:

> *If you sinful people know how to give good gifts to your children, how much more will your heavenly Father give good gifts to those who ask him.*

What this promise teaches me is that God is a perfect father who loves giving good gifts to those who go on asking him. Well, prophecy is a really good gift. Used responsibly, it brings comfort to believers and conviction to unbelievers. That sounds like something that every believer needs.

With simple, childlike faith I have been praying that the Father would strengthen the gift of prophecy in my life, my family and my church. On a daily basis I have been coming before the Father and asking him to sharpen the gift of prophecy in my own life and to pour out a great wave of the prophetic upon the church I serve.

I am writing now in August 2003. On the last three Sunday nights both of those prayers have started to be answered. A month ago the Lord told me to teach the people in St Andrew's everything that I had learned about prophetic evangelism. He also told me to take the risk and step out in faith. So I have aimed to prophesy more frequently and publicly over people in the congregation. I have also been encouraging the whole church to have a go as well. The results have been really exciting. The authority and accuracy of words over complete strangers have caused the level of faith to increase in an unprecedented way. Everyone is beginning to realise that they can prophesy. The effects on the church in terms of health and growth have been wonderful.

So dare to ask God for more of the prophetic! And keep on asking.

Third, Maintain a Constant State of Readiness

One of my favourite examples of prophetic evangelism is Jesus' encounter with Zacchaeus. This episode in Luke 19:1–10 teaches us three vital, practical principles in prophetic evangelism. They can be summed up in the three words *stop, look*, and *listen*.

First of all, STOP! The passage introduces us to the two main characters in verses 1 and 2:

> *Jesus entered Jericho and made his way through the town. There was a man there named Zacchaeus. He was one of the most influential Jews in the Roman tax-collecting business, and he had become very rich.*

The second character, Zacchaeus, was not a pleasant man. He was a Jew whose name literally meant 'righteous one'. Yet he was far from righteous. He had become successful and rich by collecting taxes from his fellow Jews and giving them to the Roman authorities. He had become a very rich businessman at others' expense. In fact, he was so successful that he became the chief tax collector in the locality. Zacchaeus was a nasty piece of work. He was a little man who compensated for lack of physical stature through the exercise of power.

Yet Jesus, the main character in the story, is about to stop for Zacchaeus. Jesus, who is en route to Jerusalem via Jericho, stops his journey for Zacchaeus. This is because Jesus never wrote anyone off. Jesus was prepared to stop a crowd for a blind beggar on the way in to Jericho (Lk. 18:35–43) and a rich tax collector on the way through Jericho. Jesus was prepared to *stop*.

Second, he was prepared to *look*. What happens next is interesting.

> *He tried to get a look at Jesus, but he was too short to see over the crowds. So he ran ahead and climbed a sycamore tree beside the road, so he could watch from there (Lk. 19:3–4).*

Zacchaeus hears that Jesus is passing by. He climbs a sycamore fig tree and hides in the branches, hoping to catch a glimpse of Jesus. The Hebrew word for the tree he's hiding in can be translated 'rehabilitation'. There's a nice irony! The point I am making, however, is this. Jesus is leading a large crowd of people but he is also looking out for the person or people that the Father wants him to stop for. Even though Zacchaeus is concealed, he cannot hide from Jesus. Just as Jesus saw Nathanael, so he sees Zacchaeus. Jesus was prepared to *look* for those looking for him.

Third, he was prepared to *listen*. Jesus listened to what the Father was saying. It must have been very noisy, but Jesus engaged in spiritual listening. He hears what the Father is saying. He hears what Zacchaeus' name is. He hears what he must call Zacchaeus to do:

> *When Jesus came by, he looked up at Zacchaeus and called him by name. 'Zacchaeus!' he said. 'Quick, come down! For I must be a guest in your home today.' Zacchaeus quickly climbed down and took Jesus to his house in great excitement and joy. But the crowds were displeased. 'He has gone to be the guest of a notorious sinner,' they grumbled (Lk. 19:5–7).*

The people grumble as they see Jesus singling out Zacchaeus in this prophetic way. But Zacchaeus is overjoyed. Jesus has called him by name. He is the Good Shepherd who calls his sheep by name and leads them out (Jn. 10:3). Zacchaeus has never met Jesus before, yet Jesus knows him *by name*. More than that, Jesus wants to come to *his* house. There must have been many more important homes to visit in Jericho. But Jesus says, 'I choose you, Zacchaeus, and I choose your home.'

The consequences of Jesus' use of prophecy in evangelism are astounding:

> *Meanwhile, Zacchaeus stood there and said to the Lord, 'I will*

give half my wealth to the poor, Lord, and if I have
overcharged people on their taxes, I will give them back four
times as much!' Jesus responded, 'Salvation has come to this
home today, for this man has shown himself to be a son of
Abraham. And I, the Son of Man, have come to seek and save
those like him who are lost' (Lk. 19:8–10).

The fruit is quite simply repentance, and this repentance
is radical. It goes way beyond what the rabbis of the day
would have required. The rabbis only asked that twenty
per cent of one's income be given to the poor. Zacchaeus
promises fifty per cent. If you overcharged someone, the
rabbis required that you pay back the same, plus one-
fifth. Zacchaeus promises four times what he has
extorted. This repentance is public, radical and saving.
What seemed impossible in Luke 18:18–30 has become
possible in Luke 19:1–10: a rich man has been saved.

What does the example of Jesus teach us? It teaches us
that we need to be prepared to stop, look and listen
every day. This means maintaining a constant state of
readiness. The devil tries to distract us daily with hurry,
crowds and noise. The person who wants to engage in
prophetic evangelism must be prepared to stop in the
hurry of their day, to look for the seeker in the crowd,
and to listen to God in the midst of noise. Zacchaeus'
conversion is a particularly powerful encouragement to
Christians in business to stop, look and listen.

Fourth, Start by Ministering to Believers First

One thing that we have emphasized at every prophetic
evangelism conference is the importance of practising
with believers before ministering to unbelievers. This has

meant that our conferences, over a weekend, have had the following schedule:

Friday eve   Introduction to Prophetic Evangelism
Saturday a.m.   How to Witness Prophetically
Saturday a.m.   Prophecy Clinic
Saturday p.m.   a. Intercession in Church
                    b. Evangelism on the Streets
Saturday eve   Testimonies and Teaching

What we have found over the last few years is that the third session, the prophecy clinic, is the most important. In that session we encourage everyone to hear from God and to speak out what they receive. This might involve forming small groups of four or five people who do not know each other, encouraging each person to stand in the middle, and everyone to prophesy. Or it might involve getting a number of people to the front and have everyone in the auditorium give prophetic words for those standing. Whatever way is chosen, the idea is to get believers to grow in confidence.

The reason for this is because there is a close relationship between our faith level and our ability to hear God's voice. Paul says this in Romans 12:6:

God has given each of us the ability to do certain things well. So if God has given you the ability to prophesy, speak out when you have faith that God is speaking through you.

The key to prophecy is to have 'faith that God is speaking through you'. Having faith means believing that God wants to speak to you and daring to share thoughts, impressions, pictures and so on with others. As you see the accuracy and impact of these prophetic insights, your faith grows accordingly.

As believers become more confident in the worship place, they become more confident in the market place. Once they realise that God really does speak to them when they are with fellow believers, they are more prepared to believe that he might speak to them when among those who don't know Jesus.

I think of Corrie, a young woman in our church. I took her as part of a team to help me run a prophetic evangelism conference in the UK. She had doubts about whether prophecy was really for her, so she decided to help my teenage daughter, Hannah, run my tape and book stall at the back. At the end of the Saturday morning session we were all waiting on God when the Holy Spirit spoke to her. She ran to the front and asked if she could give a word. The word concerned a woman present who had been a missionary to China, who had not been to that nation for a few years, but had received an opportunity to go back to China in the summer. Well, there was indeed a woman present who had been a missionary to China. She had not been back for several years but she had received an invitation that summer to go and work in an orphanage in China. She had specifically come to that conference asking God to guide her. She testified at the end of the day that Corrie's word had been just what she needed.

That encouraged Corrie. So I took her as part of a team to Canada to do a similar conference. When we came to the Saturday afternoon, teams went out to the local shopping malls. Corrie saw a woman running a stall on her own and had a word for her. She went and shared it. It was absolutely bang on! The woman was from Vietnam and not a Christian. Corrie went off and bought her a Bible, having talked to her about Jesus!

You see how it works? We build confidence and grow faith with each other in the worship place and then we dare to minister prophetically in the market place. As we are faithful in the little things that God gives us with each other, he gives us bigger things to share with those who don't know him. As Jesus said, 'Well done, good and faithful servant! You have been faithful with a few things; I will put you in charge of many things. Come and share your master's happiness!' (Mt. 25:21, NIV).

Fifth, Be Obedient to What God Tells You

Those who want to engage in prophetic evangelism need to be obedient as well as full of faith. Obedience simply means doing what the Holy Spirit tells you to do, even when you don't feel like it.

When I think of obedience I think of Philip in Acts 8:26–40. He has just conducted a hugely successful city mission in Samaria. Many people have come to Christ and the power of God has been much in evidence as unbelievers are saved, healed and delivered. But as soon as that mission ends, Philip – who has effectively been doing mass evangelism – is sent out to minister in the desert to just one man, and an Ethiopian eunuch at that:

> *As for Philip, an angel of the Lord said to him, 'Go south down the desert road that runs from Jerusalem to Gaza.' So he did, and he met the treasurer of Ethiopia, a eunuch of great authority under the queen of Ethiopia. The eunuch had gone to Jerusalem to worship, and he was now returning. Seated in his carriage, he was reading aloud from the book of the prophet Isaiah (Acts 8:26–28).*

Once again we see the importance of the prophetic in evangelism. Philip receives his directions from an angel.

'Go south to the Gaza road.' At this stage Philip is not told why he is to go there. But he is obedient, and knowing only that he must join that particular road, he goes there. When he arrives at the road he no doubt spends some time walking on it without anything happening. He must have wondered what on earth he was doing there. But then the next moment he meets a black North African eunuch in a chariot. To cut a long story short, Philip is told by the Holy Spirit to go and walk alongside the chariot. The man is a seeker and is reading a scroll of Isaiah 53, the vision of the one led like a lamb to the slaughter. Philip duly explains the meaning of that passage, telling him that the one like a lamb was Jesus. Philip then shares the Good News and the eunuch is baptised. Luke concludes the episode thus:

> *When they came up out of the water, the Spirit of the Lord caught Philip away. The eunuch never saw him again but went on his way rejoicing. Meanwhile, Philip found himself farther north at the city of Azotus! He preached the Good News there and in every city along the way until he came to Caesarea (Acts 8: 39–40).*

Philip is operating throughout this story as a prophetic evangelist. At every point his witness to the eunuch is the result of obeying the promptings of the Spirit. He obeys the instruction to go to the Gaza road even though he is not told why. He obeys the call to go alongside the chariot even though he is not told why. Philip does not question the Spirit. He simply obeys. Perhaps most revealing of all, Philip sows words into the life of a person that he never meets again. He must have wondered many times what happened to the eunuch, whether he led any fellow Ethiopians to Christ, whether a church in Africa was established when he got home. But all this is hidden from him.

Prophetic evangelism today is just like this. We obediently sow into the lives of unbelievers without necessarily knowing what ever happens. We may not ever know if they come to Christ or lead others to Christ. Much of this may remain hidden. All we do is obey what God calls *us* to do, and trust him for the rest.

In the last section I wrote about Corrie. She ministered to a Vietnamese woman in a shopping mall, giving her a word from God, and buying her a Bible. What is fascinating about this story is that Corrie went on her way wondering what would happen next. What she didn't know until the testimony time that evening is that a mother and daughter at our conference saw the same Vietnamese woman sitting with her Bible in her stall, and went and gave her some more words. They then prayed for her and told her about local churches she could join!

When we witness prophetically we are simply sowing obediently into an unbeliever's life. What happens next is up to God. The Holy Spirit may pass the baton on to someone else and it may be them, not us, that leads them to Christ. All we are called to do is *obey!*

Sixth, Guard Your Heart Against Impurity

Purity and prophecy are intimately linked. Jesus said, 'Blessed are the pure in heart, for they will see God' (Mt. 5:8, NIV). If we want to see God, we must keep our imaginations pure. We must not allow our hearts to become filled with images that are unholy. Similarly, we must take care not to allow unholy sounds and words to fill our ears, otherwise we will have problems trying to hear God's voice.

This obviously has implications for what we watch

and listen to on a day-to-day basis. I personally find that God speaks to me through movies, and I've written two books with J. John on this, entitled *The Big Picture* and *The Big Picture 2*. J. John and I have been using movie clips as visual parables with great effect for several years. At the same time, both of us would say that we have to exercise discrimination and discernment in what we see and listen to. We are both acutely aware of the dangers and neither of us wants to impair our ability to see and hear God because of impurity.

So it is extremely important to take great care to maintain a lifestyle of holiness and humility when it comes to prophetic evangelism. This is particularly important as we grow in the prophetic. We will need to guard against pride as the Lord chooses to use us. We must never allow ourselves to start thinking that we hear God with 100 per cent accuracy, that we are infallible in what we say, or that our prophecies have higher authority than the Bible. As Paul wrote in 1 Corinthians 13:12:

> *Now we see things imperfectly as in a poor mirror, but then we will see everything with perfect clarity. All that I know now is partial and incomplete, but then I will know everything completely, just as God knows me now.*

We see imperfectly in the prophetic and this will be true until Jesus returns. Then we will see perfectly, and only then. In the meantime, we must keep holy and humble.

Seventh, Cultivate Compassion for the Lost

One Sunday evening, William Booth was walking in London with his son, Bramwell, who was then twelve years old. The father surprised the son by taking him into a bar. The place was crowded with men and women, many of them bearing on their faces the marks of vice and crime; some were drunk. The fumes of alcohol and tobacco were poisonous.

'Willie,' Booth said to his son, 'these are our people; these are the people I want you to live for and bring to Christ.'

Years later, Bramwell Booth wrote, 'The impression never left me.'

We will never be truly effective in prophetic evangelism until our hearts are filled with compassion for those who don't know Christ. For Jesus, compassion was the motive for his ministry. He preached Good News to the poor not only because he was anointed but also because he was compassionate. Moved as he was by the Father's love, Jesus ministered to the crowds of lost people with a weeping heart. As Matthew records:

> *He felt great pity for the crowds that came, because their problems were so great and they didn't know where to go for help. They were like sheep without a shepherd. He said to his disciples, 'The harvest is so great, but the workers are so few. So pray to the Lord who is in charge of the harvest; ask him to send out more workers for his fields' (Mt. 9:36–38).*

As we grow in compassion for the lost, God will put people on our hearts that he wants us to pray for and witness to. There is definitely a relationship between heartfelt, compassionate pleading on behalf of the lost and opportunities for prophetic evangelism. We need to knock continuously on heaven's door on behalf of our unbelieving family, friends, neighbours and colleagues. Intercession flows out of compassion, and prophetic revelation comes to those who pray.

Eighth, Don't Let the Enemy Stop You

The enemy always lies to people that prophecy is for the super-spiritual elite, but this is completely false. Philippians 4:13 says, 'For I can do everything with the help of Christ who gives me the strength I need.'

A prophetic evangelism conference in the UK proved the point for me. There was a church elder present at a day I led who was happy to support the prophetic but was convinced that he himself could not prophesy. Unknown to him, his pastor was praying that day that God would really show him that he could indeed prophesy.

As we formed into groups of four or five after lunch, this elder, before he even knew what he was doing, said the following to a complete stranger: 'Your name is Anne. You have been working all your life with handicapped children. You have just retired and you have come here today asking God whether you should continue in a voluntary capacity. And the Lord says, "Yes!"'

Every single word of that prophecy was completely accurate, even down to the name Anne. Needless to say, the woman started weeping. She had heard God's voice clearer than she could ever have imagined possible. The elder started crying too. He was simply overwhelmed that God could have used him in this way.

Many of us are held back from operating in the gift of prophecy, either in the church or outside. Chief among the reasons is the lie that says we can't do it. In addition to this, the enemy plays on fear. We are afraid of letting God down, of not hearing him, of hearing him incorrectly, of causing an embarrassment, of saying the wrong thing, or of not having the words.

The truth is, sometimes we may get it wrong, but it says in Proverbs 24:16 that 'though a righteous man falls seven times, he rises again' (NIV). We need to remember that we are far more fearful of giving a word than an unbeliever is of receiving one! So we must not allow the enemy to immobilise us in the area of prophetic evangelism. He wants to kill the prophetic in us through lies and fear. He is a robber who wants to steal this gift from the church. We are called to resist him.

Ninth, Let Testimony Increase Expectancy

The reason I have included so many testimonies of prophetic evangelism in this book is not because I am trying to prove something. Rather, I want to raise your level of expectation that God might speak through you to an unbeliever. Faith comes by hearing, and in this book you have heard many stories of people who have received revelation with life-changing consequences. My prayer is that this has greatly increased your level of expectancy as regards your own walk with God.

Testimonies from the Bible, from church history and from people's experience today are vital. One of our mottoes in church leadership is 'celebrate what you want to propagate'. I want to propagate a church full of people who are witnessing prophetically to the lost, in our community and beyond. For that reason I use testimonies in my preaching that are carefully chosen not only to illustrate biblical points but also to raise awareness and expectancy in the church. Similarly, I am constantly on the alert for testimonies from Christians who are living ordinary lives but who are being used in extraordinary ways in prophetic evangelism. When I hear of such people, either in my church or in another church, I will get them to share their story publicly so that all may be encouraged.

The great thing about having housewives, business people, flight attendants, policemen and teachers sharing their experiences is that people in the church more readily identify with them than with vicars and professional evangelists. When people from regular walks of life share their testimonies, people are much more likely to say, 'Yes, I can relate to that.'

Don't get me wrong. I am not saying that vicars and evangelists aren't normal! But those of us in these professions know that our stories can have only limited relevance because we live very unusual lifestyles.

So, I would encourage you to look out for those testimonies that build faith in God's power to speak prophetically to unbelievers.

Tenth, Get Close to Anointed Practitioners

This is so important too. Jesus mentored the disciples in prophetic evangelism, which is one reason why we see them witnessing prophetically in the book of Acts. They had been close to an anointed practitioner.

I am a church leader and so people look to me as an expert on spiritual matters. But I realised some years ago that the Lord was saying he was going to use prophecy in evangelism in an unprecedented way. As I heard him saying that, I also felt very weak. Using prophecy in evangelism was not my personal strength at that time.

Realising these two things, I set about looking for those who were already 'anointed practitioners'. I found one who exercised a full-time ministry as an itinerant prophet. I listened to what he had to say, read everything he wrote on the subject, and went to meet him. At the same time, I began to realise that there were several people in my church who were already moving in this ministry. One of these worked as a businessman and the other was a British Airways flight attendant. Both of these had wanted for a long time to use prophecy in evangelism, and both were already doing the stuff. One was using it at 35,000 feet with passengers and crew on board an aircraft. The other was using it here at ground level with fellow business people.

I decided to invest in relationships with church members like these, not only because I really like them but also because I know I have a lot to learn. In a sense, I submitted myself to an unofficial process of mentoring, certainly with one of them. This has involved on one occasion going out with him into a city to evangelise, learning what I can by watching and listening. I did this because I wanted to get close to an anointed practitioner.

Mentoring is therefore vital. This applies even to people in our own family. The Bible says that your sons and daughters shall prophesy (Acts 2:17). I recognise that I have a responsibility to mentor my four children in prophetic evangelism, so I take the older ones with me on conferences, here and abroad. Indeed, it has been wonderful to see them grow in this ministry.

Demonstrations of God's Power

It takes time to learn how to hear what God is saying about unbelievers and it takes time to learn how to share it in a way that leads to life-change. Applying the ten practical steps in this chapter will be a start. If you commit yourself to a process of learning you will find that God speaks to you more and more and that lost people are more and more impacted as you speak to them. But it will take time. In an instant culture, we need to recognise that spiritual formation does not take place immediately but over a long period of time.

All of us desire to have a greater impact on those who do not yet know Jesus. At the same time, we realise that trying to evangelise others in our own strength just doesn't seem to have any lasting influence. What we really need is what Paul described as 'demonstrations' or 'proofs' of the Spirit's power. Paul's method of evangelism involved not only sharing about what Jesus had done on the Cross but also demonstrating the truth of the Gospel through signs, wonders and miracles. This is how he put it in 1 Corinthians 2:1–5:

> *Dear brothers and sisters, when I first came to you I didn't use lofty words and brilliant ideas to tell you God's message. For I decided to concentrate only on Jesus Christ and his death on the cross. I came to you in weakness – timid and trembling. And my message and my preaching were very plain. I did not use wise and persuasive speeches, but the Holy Spirit was powerful among you. I did this so that you might trust the power of God rather than human wisdom.*

Most of us could probably be a lot more proficient at explaining the significance of 'Jesus Christ and his death on the Cross' (v. 2). I have written a whole book on the Cross from a charismatic perspective, called *Fire and Blood*. This may be a help if you need more training in understanding and communicating the message of the Cross, especially to those who do not yet believe.

At the same time, nearly all of us, I suspect, desire to see more of God's power at work in and through our lives. We know that God can do immeasurably more than we could ever ask or imagine, according to the power that is already at work in us (Eph. 3:20). We know that there is so much more of that mighty power that raised Jesus from the dead for us to experience (Eph. 1:19–20). We know this because the Bible tells us so. Yet, we seem to experience so little. The gap between what the Bible says and what we actually experience is a great one.

What we desperately need is more of God's power.

And we need to see it, not just talk about it. We need personal knowledge, not just theoretical knowledge. Proclamation is one thing. Demonstration is another. What we need is more proofs of the Spirit's power in our mission to those who don't know Jesus Christ. The gift of prophecy is one such demonstration or 'proof'. A lost person exposed to the voice of God knows from that moment on that God is real and that he knows them personally. The effects of that realisation are, sooner or later, seismic. In order for us to be used in this kind of way we need to see God's power and point to it. We need an up-to-date testimony of what the Holy Spirit is saying and doing in our lives.

I have used a lot of stories in this book, all of them true. This book has in fact been something of a 'narrative theology'. As a charismatic, I believe (like the Pentecostals) that testimony is vital. Stories of what God is doing confirm the truth of what God has already said in his Word.

So let me end with another testimony.

A friend of mine was in a restaurant with a work colleague. She was explaining who the Holy Spirit is and what the Holy Spirit does. Evidently the colleague was very curious about this. As they were talking, two men came and sat at the same table and joined them. They all engaged in conversation. One of them had to leave a little later and said, 'I have to go now and meet my wife.' His companion looked at him and said, 'I didn't know you were married. Do you have any children?'

At that moment, my friend, having never met him before, looked at him and said, 'Yes, he has an eighteen-month-old daughter called Jessica.'

The man was astounded. 'Do I know you?' he asked.

'No,' my friend replied.

'Then how did you know about my daughter?'

'It doesn't matter,' she said.

The man left to go and meet his wife. As soon as he had gone, my friend turned to her work colleague and said, 'That's what the Holy Spirit does . . .'

CONCLUSION

The last thought I'd like to leave you with is about leadership.

Leading a church is one of the most demanding vocations there is. The calls on your time are endless and the task occupies your thoughts 24/7. Often leaders are driven by pressures rather than governed by priorities. In the process, tirelessly maintaining structures, fulfilling basic duties and constantly pastoring those already in the church takes up every hour in the day. Barely is there time to have a conversation with members of your own family, let alone a non-Christian on the streets.

And this is where I believe things have to change. Leaders need to be set free to lead. Indeed, I see a day coming when leaders will *have* to be set free to lead. If all they have time for is maintenance, they will end up burnt out and the churches will continue to decline until they are empty. Leaders need to be given time to develop vision and they need to be allowed to be pioneers, not settlers.

My final word is therefore to those who find themselves as leaders of churches, Christian organisations and departments, ministries and groups.

My conviction is that the Holy Spirit is going to do a major work of transition in the lives of people in pastoral leadership. What is the transition going to be *from*? What is it going to be *to*?

Last December I faced a challenge that I guess most senior pastors faced: preparing fresh messages on the Christmas story. Those of you who don't have this responsibility will never know what a problem this can be. The Christmas story is the most familiar of all, and for those of us who have been in church leadership for several decades, it is extremely hard to see anything new.

Having said that, as I prepared a message entitled 'The Shepherd's Delight', the Lord really spoke to me out of Luke chapter 2. As I read these very familiar words, I sensed the Holy Spirit showing me that the change experienced by the shepherds in this story is going to be experienced by shepherds or pastors in the churches:

That night some shepherds were in the fields outside the village, guarding their flocks of sheep. Suddenly, an angel of the Lord appeared among them, and the radiance of the Lord's glory surrounded them. They were terribly frightened, but the angel reassured them. 'Don't be afraid!' he said. 'I bring you good news of great joy for everyone! The Saviour – yes, the Messiah, the Lord – has been born tonight in Bethlehem, the city of David! And this is how you will recognise him: You will find a baby lying in a manger, wrapped snugly in strips of cloth!' Suddenly, the angel was joined by a vast host of others – the armies of heaven – praising God: 'Glory to God in the highest heaven and peace on earth to all whom God favours.' When the angels had returned to heaven, the shepherds said to each other, 'Come on, let's go to Bethlehem! Let's see this wonderful thing that has happened, which the Lord has told us about.' They ran to the village and found Mary and Joseph. And there was the baby, lying in the manger. Then the shepherds told everyone what had happened and what the angel had said to them about this child. All who heard the shepherds' story were astonished, but Mary quietly treasured these things in her heart and thought about them often. The shepherds went back to their fields and flocks, glorifying and praising God for what the angels had told them, and because they had seen the child, just as the angel had said (Lk. 2: 8–20).

This is a great passage! Here the shepherds are given a major revelation of the glory of God. An angel announces the Good News of the Saviour's birth. A chorus of angels then appears in the heavens, giving glory to God in the highest.

Now it's what happens next that I find so illuminating. The shepherds had been in their familiar fields playing their pipes, watching their sheep, and looking out for bears and thieves. But as soon as the angel announces the Saviour's birth they run from those fields with an extraordinary excitement. They leave their sheep in the fields, much as Moses did in Exodus 3, when he too experienced a revelation from God:

> *One day Moses was tending the flock of his father-in-law, Jethro, the priest of Midian, and he went deep into the wilderness near Sinai, the mountain of God. Suddenly, the angel of the LORD appeared to him as a blazing fire in a bush. Moses was amazed because the bush was engulfed in flames, but it didn't burn up. 'Amazing!' Moses said to himself. 'Why isn't that bush burning up? I must go over to see this' (Ex. 3: 1–3).*

Just as Moses was so captivated by the glory of God that he left his sheep, so are the shepherds in Luke 2.

So what happens next? The shepherds run to Bethlehem, leaving the sheep on the hills, and they meet the baby Jesus in the manger. This so enthrals them that they do something very unexpected for a shepherd. Luke reports in verse 17: 'Then the shepherds told everyone what had happened and what the angel had said to them about this child.'

See what has happened here. The shepherds have turned into heralds. They declare the news about Jesus and everyone who heard them is filled with awe.

What is the significance of this?

I believe we are entering a season when those who are currently in a pastoral role are going to be so excited about Jesus that they turn from shepherds into heralds.

My experience is that most people who are pastors really have the heart of an evangelist. Deep down they want to be set free to share the Gospel with the lost. This is how most pastors started their Christians lives. Yet somehow they have become immersed in maintenance and have no time for mission.

In the season that is coming, leaders are going to start leading. They are going to be set free from many of the administrative and pastoral demands that have prevented them from fulfilling their pioneering calling. Other people are going to be called by God to rise up and take on those responsibilities. Meanwhile, leaders are going to start enjoying their ministry again. They are going to have the evangelistic part of their hearts renewed. That heavy burden that says, 'I never have time to witness to non-Christians' is going to go. Shepherds are going to become heralds. Pastors are going to become evangelists. For many this transition will lead to a great renewal of vision and hope.

What I sensed the Holy Spirit saying out of my study of Luke 2 was simply this:

'Tell pastors that they are going to experience major transition in their ministries. Many have been stuck in one particular field of influence watching over those who are already in the fold. You have done this faithfully and obediently, yet at the same time there has been a holy frustration in your heart. You have been crying out to yourself, "There has to be more than this." This message is from heaven and it is for *you*! I am going to take you in these coming years out of your field and give you a fresh enthusiasm for the person of my Son. It is in fact going to be like it was at the beginning for many of you. I am going to renew your first love and birth my Son afresh in your hearts. Out of the fullness of this revelation, I am going to cause you to move from being a pastor alone to being a pastor-evangelist – shepherds who cannot stop themselves going out of their comfort zones to declare who Jesus really is. As you do this, I will raise up others to look after the sheep so that you will be free to go after lost sheep rather than focus on those who have been found. As you do this, you will rediscover joy in service and a fresh passion for pastoring will come upon you as you return to the flock. As you see new faces, you will rejoice in what I, the Lord, have done.

'So take heart. These are indeed years of transition. Some of you have always been pastors with an evangelist's heart. In these days I will reactivate what has become dormant and you will experience a new release of evangelistic passion and anointing. But this is my message to you. Do not think that your ministry is always going to be like this. Prepare yourself for change. Look for those to whom you can delegate the shepherd's tasks. Seek after a fresh revelation of Jesus that will compel you to declare the wonders of my Son.'

Why have I ended on this note? The answer is simple. The church will never fulfil its calling to prophetic evangelism while its leaders are so imprisoned in the church that they never even see a non-Christian. Churches *must* release their pastors to have more time to form relationships with unbelievers and to witness to them, especially in the communities where they live and work. No leader is going to lead their church into prophetic evangelism if they themselves are unable to find any time to develop their own testimonies. Even a man like Timothy, whose work was mainly pastoral, was exhorted by the Apostle Paul to do the work of an evangelist (2 Tim. 4:5). Timothy was not primarily called to be an evangelist but a pastor, yet he was told to do the work of an evangelist. The same is true for those in pastoral leadership today.

If you are in pastoral leadership, my prayer is that God will not only increase the prophetic in your life, but also renew the evangelistic part of your calling. In this way, you and I will become contagious leaders – leading our people from consumerism to evangelism. The days that lie ahead of us will require missionary leaders. So may our heavenly Father send the Holy Spirit afresh into every church leader's heart, releasing a new passion for Jesus and a deep compassion for the lost.

APPENDIX 1

Guidelines for the Exercise of Prophecy
St Andrew's Church, Chorleywood

We understand prophecy to be a revelation about a person or a situation, given by the Holy Spirit, and spoken out for the benefit of others. We expect these words to be in the form of a message, a statement, a vision, a picture, a passage of Scripture, an impression and/or a sensation. We value the gift of prophecy and welcome the prophetic in St Andrew's. We teach that every believer can prophesy, and we seek to encourage everyone to 'have a go', and at the same time to be accountable to the leadership. Therefore we require everyone (including ourselves) to observe these guidelines:

1. We believe that the spirit of prophecy is the testimony of Jesus, so we look to glorify Jesus Christ and not ourselves through the use of this gift.
2. We urge that 'prepared' prophecies – especially correctional prophecies about the church – should be submitted to the leadership before they are uttered.
3. We ask people to speak prophetic words clearly, briefly, calmly and lovingly, on the basis that the spirit of the prophet is subject to the control of the prophet.

4. We also ask people to be wary of prophesying about subjects in which they have a personal, emotional involvement.

5. We only allow those who are members of St Andrew's to give prophecies out loud (for the sake of ongoing accountability), though we encourage visitors to write down any words they receive and to send them to us.

6. We seek to pause after two or three words have been given in order to weigh what has been said, before continuing with more words if appropriate.

7. We believe that genuine prophecies are to strengthen, encourage and comfort God's people.

8. We actively discourage directional or manipulative prophecies (i.e. words that tell people what to do with their lives, health, relationships, jobs and so on, in the future).

9. We urge people to offer words with humility and to think of prefacing their comments with 'I sense the Lord may be saying . . .' rather than 'Thus says the Lord . . .'.

10. We believe that character is as important as charisma, and therefore we reserve the right to ask those who are struggling with character issues (particularly sin issues) not to prophesy until the matter in question is resolved.

11. We recognize that God allows his gifts to dwell in imperfect people and that prophetic giftedness is not necessarily a sign of superior holiness or of a closer relationship with the Lord.

12. We remember that our value to God lies in the fact that we are loved and accepted as his children, and not because we prophesy well or badly.

13. We believe in encouraging and training people to

grow in their prophetic gifts so that they can reach deeper levels of maturity and ministry.

14. We believe that prophets are accountable to their leadership and that once they have delivered a word they have relinquished ownership of it and responsibility for it.

15. We hold fast to the view that prophecy is subject to Scripture, not Scripture to prophecy, and in the light of this we urge people to put the Bible first.

16. We welcome interpretations of words of revelation from the body, and ask that these be written out and placed in the prophecy box in the vestibule.

APPENDIX 2

**Dream Teams at the Manchester Games, 2002:
a report by Doug Addison**

City streets buzzed with excitement as more than one
million visitors poured into Manchester, England, for the
biggest sporting event in British history. Fans of the 17th
Commonwealth Games swarmed athletics venues,
restaurants, pubs and coffee shops. Revellers celebrated
nightly until the early hours of the morning.

Inside Starbucks, a crowd of people stood in line for
iced lattes and mocha frapps to offset the balmy
afternoon heat. Meanwhile in the back corner, a small
group gathered around two tables that displayed a sign,
'Free Dream Interpretation.' After listening to a few
dreams being interpreted, those sitting nearby jumped
up to share their dreams with the Streams Dream Team.

A practising Muslim shared a recurring dream. As a
spiritual interpretation was offered along with a
prophetic word from the Lord, the woman seemed
deeply touched. Confused how strangers could know
such things about her, the woman exclaimed, 'I have to
know more about this God!'

Another Muslim kept repeating, 'I cannot believe that
you are Christians because you are so kind to me.'

'As I was interpreting a dream,' remembers Anna
Ashford from Orlando, Florida, 'the Lord began to reveal
information about the woman's family and how she felt

toward them. The woman was stunned. Even though she did not believe in Jesus, I shared that he is where all true revelation comes from.'

The Streams Dream Teams had been invited to Manchester by Calvary International Ministries, an inner-city black church that primarily ministers to the Nigerian community. Their pastor had learned about the Streams outreach at the Winter Olympics and was eager for his church to host a similar outreach at the Commonwealth Games.

With overflowing hearts of joy and gratitude, this little church with a global vision provided housing and local transportation for the all-white, 14-member Streams Dream Team. Although Dream Team members had travelled from different geographic regions of the US and represented different denominational backgrounds, they were unified by a common vision to see God draw people to himself through the use of dreams and visions.

After an orientation to the area and training in sharing God's love prophetically, members were divided into three teams for the remaining five days of outreaches. Morning outreaches were usually held at various Starbucks coffee shops, and at night, Dream Teams made their way into local pubs.

'At one pub, a young woman sat down saying, "I want to be spiritually cleansed,"' remembers Cindy McGill, who along with her husband pastors a church in Salt Lake City, Utah. 'We began to share God's heart toward her and his faithfulness in our lives. Interrupting me, she asked, "How can I experience this?" I was amazed by her hunger for God.'

Amazingly, a month prior to the prophetic outreach event, Brenda Varela from New York had dreamed of being in downtown Manchester, seeing a library and behind it a parked car with the words 'Austin Powers' on its side. To everyone's surprise, she began screaming, 'Stop!' as her mind flashed back to her dream. 'Suddenly, I was in my dream, where I had walked those very streets,' recalls Brenda. 'It was the wildest thing I've ever experienced. I asked the pastor if there was a library nearby. As he pointed at it, I asked him to drive behind it. To our amazement, there was a black taxi with a sign on its side saying, "Austin Powers". Suddenly, we knew that God was going to give us a divine appointment – which he did!'

Strangely enough, Scott Evelyn, from West Milford, New Jersey, who was in the car with Brenda, had also had a previous dream about a building adjacent to the library. 'It was an unnerving experience,' explained Scott. 'I had the feeling that I'd literally been there a year before in my dream. It was a little scary. God seemed to be highlighting that area of Manchester to us. Our expectation of seeing God miraculously was very high.'

On the last day of the trip, as team members gathered together at the town centre to say goodbye, Jacquelyne Davidson, from Dunfermline, Scotland, shared her disappointment about not meeting someone named Martin whom she had dreamed about. It was the only thing that hadn't come to pass.

Suddenly, in an amazing turn of events, two men walked up to the group and began asking what was going on. One of them said, 'Hey, my name is Martin.' Everyone went wild.

'As I shared my dream with Martin, he was totally stunned to discover that God was calling out to him,' recalls Jacquelyne. After hearing the dream, Martin gave his heart to Jesus.

'The Streams Dream Teams has helped change the

spiritual atmosphere in my church and in the city of Manchester,' said Pastor Olatyoe. 'I was delighted to see how open people were to hearing a prophetic word from God and how easy it was to speak God's love into their lives.'

Reprinted from *AWE Magazine*, Fall 2002 issue (Streams Ministries). Used by permission.

BIBLIOGRAPHY

Books Quoted

Collins, Bruce, *Prophesy*, Berkhamsted, Herts, UK, New Wine Publications, 2000

Dunn, J.E., *Jesus and the Spirit*, London, SCM Press, 1975

Grudem, W., *The Gift of Prophecy in the New Testament and Today*, revised edn, Illinois, Crossway Books, 2000

Randolph, L., *User Friendly Prophecy: Insights and Guidelines For the Effective Use of Spiritual Gifts*, Century City, CA, Cherith Publications, 1995

Stibbe, M., *Know Your Spiritual Gifts*, London, Hodder & Stoughton, 1997

Stibbe, M., *Fire and Blood: The Work of the Spirit, the Work of the Cross*, London, Monarch, 2001

Stibbe, M. and J. John, *The Big Picture: Finding the Spiritual Message in Movies*, Milton Keynes, Authentic Lifestyle, 2002

Stibbe, M., *The Teacher's Notebook*, Eastbourne, Kingsway, 2003

Wright, J., *The Desert Road South of Jerusalem*, Norwich, The Branch Press, 2003

Courses Quoted

Stone, S., *Apostolic Prophetic Evangelism: Compelling Them to Come*, Teacher's Manual, Christian International Europe, 2002

Web Articles Quoted

Doug Addison, 'Prophetic Evangelism',
　　at http://www.dougaddison.com/articles/prophetic
　　evangelism.html
Anonymous, 'Dreams and Visions of Jesus by Muslims'
　　at http://www.isaalmasih.net/isa/dreamsofisa.html
John Paul Jackson, 'Are we Creating Christian Psychics?'
　　at http://www.streamsministries.com/
　　April2002.html
Steve Witt, 'The Lost Art of Prophetic Evangelism',
　　at http://www.tacf.org/stf/archive/2-4/
　　prophet.html

Web Sites Consulted

Alister Hardy Religious Experience Research Centre
　　Archive
http://www.archiveshub.ac.uk/news/ahrerca.html

For Details of Mark Stibbe's Other Resources:

Contact:
Alie Stibbe
Word & Spirit Resources Ltd
37 Quickley Lane
Chorleywood
Herts
UK
WD3 5AE
Or aliestibbe@aol.com
(Word & Spirit Resources Ltd is a registered company:
No. 4396221)